Love, Mum ox
Easter 2018

PALL OF SILENCE

My Journey from Tragedy to Trust

"Shall not the Judge of all the Earth do right?" (Gen. 18:25)

Eleanor Bertin

Eleanor Bertin

In honour of Paul's early fascination with languages, a portion of royalties from this book will be donated to Wycliffe Bible Translators.

Published by Discern Products
724 Parkdale Ave.
Ottawa, Ontario, Canada K1Y 1J6
info@discernproducts.com
www.discernproducts.com

Cover photo is of Paul Bertin and taken by Thomas James Bertin, thetigerfactory.com
Cover design by Donald Marsanic
Author photo: Alyssa Raeanne Photography, alyssaraeanne.ca

ISBN 978 1-988422-12-1

Printed by Gauvin Press
Gatineau, Québec

In memory of

Paul Gabriel Bertin

May 7, 1994 – October 6, 2012

"Jesus said to her, 'I am the resurrection and the life.

He who believes in Me, though he may die, he shall live.

And whoever lives and believes in Me shall never die"

John 11:25, 26

Chapter 1 – Police at the Door

October 6, 2012

It wasn't the kind of thing you longed for – emergency vehicle lights flashing blue and red through your front window and reflecting against the kitchen appliances in the early dark of an autumn morning. What you longed for, without even realizing it, was the bland, the familiar, the blessed boring.

Like leaves falling from the trees, I expected to count off the three days of the Thanksgiving weekend of 2012 in the usual renovation work, housework and of course, preparation for a big family meal after church on Sunday. The most excitement I longed for was the anticipation of being joined for turkey dinner by our family.

So, when we stood owl-eyed at the front door, me in my worn green housecoat, my husband in his hastily donned T-shirt and jeans, trying to take in the brutal facts the officer was stating, I resisted change with everything in me. I couldn't begin to fathom the depths to which my soul would ultimately plummet. As it was, the force of such an impact kept me falling, falling – dangling in a dense fog of unreality for many months.

I had been awakened that morning by the fax ring and drowsily thought I should probably discontinue the service. Our high school son, Paul, had graduated and wouldn't be using it to contact his teachers anymore. I got up to go to the bathroom and noticed the time – 4:55 a.m. It was when I opened the door of our room that I saw the flashing lights. Their garish swirling from outside streaked around the dining room and kitchen. At that hour I didn't want to be answering the door alone so I shook my husband awake. Grumpily, Mike pulled on some pants, disgusted at being awakened too early on a weekend. Both our dogs were barking and now there was banging on the dining room French doors at the side of the house. We opened the front door to find two women and an RCMP officer standing below our steps, keeping their distance from the dogs. Living half an hour from town, we rarely see police, so the sight of the uniform immediately set me trembling. Settling the animals, we motioned to the visitors to come up.

"We're investigating a hit and run pedestrian fatality…" the officer began.

At that, my heart plunged into a bottomless void. *Oh no! One of my boys has done something!* My mind flashed back to a message one of them had sent me months earlier, stating he had been drunk and driving for quite some time on the wrong side of the road. And I thought of his younger brother Paul, a relatively new driver with an insistently heavy foot. I'd constantly had to remind him to slow down. *My boys! What have you done?* Mike told me later the same thoughts had gone through his mind.

Then the word *fatality* got through to me. *Fatality means someone died! Oh no, OH NO! This means they've killed someone! My boys will live with that guilt for the rest of their lives!*

"Is your son home?" the officer continued.

"Which one?" Mike asked.

I, too, was confused by the question. We have six sons, Ben, Dan, Tommy, Jonny, Paul and Timothy. The oldest, Ben, was married to Christy and lived in Tallahassee where he was pursuing a doctorate in piano at Florida State University. Dan was next, newly married to Courtney and living in town just half an hour away but at the time, working for an oilfield transport company up north in Peace River, Alberta. Number three, Tommy, roomed with his brother Jonny in Red Deer, Alberta, and both worked for a fencing company. It was with these two that 18-year-old Paul had been staying since mid-August, working in the fencing industry as well. Our youngest son, Timothy, has Down syndrome and was then safe in our home. In the midst of all these boys, three brothers older, three younger, we also have a daughter. Becky, married to John and living in Texas, was the busy mother of our precious twin granddaughters, Abby and Victoria, then two years old.

But the officer had asked if our son was home.

"Can you describe your son?" he asked.

Too much was racing through my mind to answer. Mike managed to stammer something but the officer continued, "Green mohawk, dog collar, skinny?"

He must mean Paul. How embarrassing to have him known for green hair. Dog collar? That must be yet another new punk accessory. I wish he'd quit wasting his money on such trash. And skinny? Paul isn't skinny. Just a normal slim, masculine eighteen-year-old build. Wait! Somewhere in there the officer had used the word "deceased."

From a great distance, it seemed, I began to hear what the police officer was trying to tell us. The fatality was our son, Paul. Relief immediately washed over me. At least none of our sons had been the perpetrator of this hit-and-run crime. Better to be a victim than a criminal, I thought.

Of all things, relief? What kind of a mother feels relief upon learning of the death of her son? My husband told me later he, too, felt that way at first.

Numbly, we asked the officer and the two women who introduced themselves as representing Victim Services, to come in and sit down. The enormity of their words was far too much to take in. I sat there on the couch, a polite observer of the scene in our living room – a bath-robed statue. My thoughts slammed back and forth from the devastating to the inconsequential.

Paul was not ready to die!

Should I offer these folks coffee?

He had begun to openly resist going to church or reading the Bible!

What do these folks think of us as they look around our home? Does it look to them as though we raised our son to be a punk?

IS MY BOY IN HELL?

The officer recounted the facts. At 2:05 a.m., a passing motorist had found Paul lying in the northbound lane of the Taylor Drive Bridge in Red Deer, a city of about 90,000. She reported it to police. EMS had pronounced him dead at the scene. The Victim Services lady talked about what would happen to the body next. *The body!* It would go to Calgary to the Medical Examiner. There might or might not be an autopsy…

I struggled to absorb what they were saying, the syllables echoing from far, far away. We must have seemed utterly stupid as the officer and the women reiterated their information several times over. Were we alright, they wanted to know. Was there anyone they could call for us? Finally, leaving a Victim Services card and assuring us they would be in touch, the three of them left.

We sat silent in the dim circle of our lamp-lit living room. Enveloped by the early morning stillness we were stunned beyond anything we had ever known. It was still far too early to call our children with this news.

Mechanically, we prayed together, asking God's help in this terrible tragedy, to be with our other children, to give us understanding for the many ways people might express their grief. I even prayed retroactively, remembering that God says, "before you call, I will answer." God would consider the source, wouldn't he, a heartbroken, terrified mother? Even as I prayed, I hoped he would remember I am but dust and overlook my theological incorrectness.

Oh God, please let Paul have had some moments to repent before he died!

The anguish of not knowing his eternal destiny tore at me. I believe what the Bible teaches about hell. God would not be just if he didn't punish evil. And if he punishes great evils like torture and murder, he assuredly must punish all evil, even the little sins we so readily excuse in ourselves. But if ever there were a time I wanted to alter the message of the Bible, that was it.

In the pre-dawn darkness, my husband and I talked about how it only takes a moment, a twinkling, a fleeting thought to say, "I'm sorry God! I've been wrong! Please forgive me!"

And my husband said, "What we have to remember is that if Paul was elect, God will not have failed to save him." I knew he spoke the truth, but at the time, all I heard in that statement was a very big, very conditional, utterly terrifying ***if.***

Chapter 2 – Living the Dream

T*here is a time to be born and a time to die,* wise King Solomon once wrote.

I own a vintage 1945 Life magazine found during one of our house renovations. In it, ads for everything from shoes and soap to kitchen appliances promise hope of a peaceful life after Victory. "In your Victory kitchen, you need a Kelvinator refrigerator!" Lovers in the throes of World War II kept hope alive dreaming about the "normal" life they'd live *after* the war. He would go to his nice secure job. She would keep house in their safe, picket-fenced home. They would have children – the fruit of their trust in a safe future. A life of constancy was their promise.

Through the 80s and early 90s, we were living that dream. I had always longed for six children, although the family of my dreams would have had a more balanced mix of boys and girls. Paul was our sixth child and fifth son. On a warm spring night in May 1994, to the sound of frogs chirruping loudly outside our bedroom window, I gave birth to that nine-pound, one-ounce baby boy. The cord had been around his neck in the birth process, making him alarmingly blue. At least it seemed so to me. But the midwife was calm and confident.

"He'll pink up pretty soon," she said as she applied oxygen. And he did. It was the time to be born, not the time to die. Only looking back on that event years later, do I see the providence of God in sparing Paul's life at birth. His time had not yet come.

When she laid him on my chest, a chubby, slippery, wide-eyed scrap of humanity, he held up his head craning it to look around. None of our other children had ever done such a thing at birth. In fact, we never did have to support his head. I remember other mothers in the church nursery laughing when they noticed me laying Paul down to change his diaper. It was my routine to gently press on his forehead so that he would relax his head. Otherwise he held it erect, always on alert.

To my husband and me, that strength of his from such an early age carried import. Surely this child was destined for some sacred purpose. We didn't know what it might be, but we felt a solemn weight of responsibility for training him and teaching him in a way that would prepare him for whatever it was.

We named him Paul, meaning "small," with the idea of humility, and Gabriel, "man of God," something we prayed he would become.

"I just love Paul Gabriel's name," read one congratulatory baby card from a friend, "another treasure from heaven for you and Mike to mold and guide."

"How we rejoice with you at the birth of Paul Gabriel!" my sister wrote. "The Lord has assigned your portion and your cup, and made your lot secure (five strong sons and a daughter!). The lines have fallen for you in pleasant places; surely you have a delightful inheritance! Psalm 15: 5, 6."

"God has given Paul Gabriel to you to raise for His glory. As Paul in the New Testament was a special messenger, may your Paul be too, a light and a witness," another friend jotted in her card.

When I mentioned the meaning of Paul's names at his funeral, it was with a sense of bitter futility mingled with a guilty despair. *What had been the point of all our teaching and training? Worse than that, where had we failed him that we were left with no clear evidence of his trusting in Jesus?*

It's been my observation that highly intelligent babies can also be intense and demanding. It was through Paul, my sixth baby, that God began to slough away some of my selfishness and replace it with true patience and submission to his will. I began to learn to curb my urge to complain inwardly at the frequent night waking. When the baby still cried after I'd done all I knew to do – feeding, changing, burping, rocking, singing – I resisted the urge to lay him, screaming, beside my husband to let him take his turn. I learned to trust Jesus to give me, whom he calls his beloved, sleep in exactly the right measure, at exactly the right time as He promises in Psalm 127. If I was awake, I reasoned, it was by God's choice. So, I learned to rejoice in night feedings, if a bit groggily. I began to see the time as an opportunity to be alone with the Lord in prayer.

I suppose all parents are amazed by their children, but I remember once when Paul was about a year old, looking into his dark blue eyes as he was nursing. He stopped and gazed up at me with a look so knowing, so intense, so fathomless, I felt he was considering my very soul. What was he thinking? What did he see or know? For me, it was one of those throat-swelling, heart-tripping moments of love for my child. Could I ever convey my love for him in return? Would he ever know the intensity of that love?

But there were also stresses in each of our lives at that time that drew Mike and me to greater dependence on a sovereign God. Job loss, financial strain, starting a new business and home educating our five older growing children all served to stretch us both to our limits. I had never before felt so out of my depth or beyond my ability.

"I feel like I'm on roller-skates," I told my husband in bed one night, after rocking baby Paul to sleep, "racing from one crisis to the next all day long."

"So do I," he answered with sleep-slurred words, perhaps thinking of his business and sales pressures.

Paul was constant motion and sound in one wiry little body. A group baking or craft session with the children quickly became a frantic fiasco of flour or glue. I learned to pair the kids, older with younger, or work with them one-on-one. Paul's curiosity, continual movement and constant chatter kept me nervously on edge. When he was just past two, a simple incident revealed to me how that edginess had begun to skew my view of him.

One day in late August 1996, I'd taken all the kids to a park and put the older ones in charge of the littles. I stayed behind in our van parked on a rise overlooking the path to where the kids were playing. I spread out my notes on the dash and began planning our upcoming home school year. As I made progress I started to relax, finding a rhythm in defining the educational goals for each child, planning curriculum and drawing up a schedule.

When I looked out the windshield from my parking space, I spotted a tiny figure meandering back toward me. Sunlight gleamed off the shining blond head. The child flitted from one side of the path to the other, bending to look at something in the rough-mown grass edging the path, twirling to trace the flight of a butterfly, tossing a handful of sand in the air. *What a sweet little child!* I reminded myself that our decision to home educate had been born out of the desire to foster exactly that kind of child-like wonder. We wanted to keep our children from the unnecessary rigid confinement of institutional school, and free them to explore and interact with the world around them. Had we lost some of that wonder, creativity and freedom in the urgent press of life? Had the looming demand to prepare the older ones for higher learning dulled my enjoyment of the little ones? I looked down at my school plans wondering if I were creating a cage of rigid institutionalism of my own.

The next time I looked up, the child was nearer – a little golden-haired boy in overalls and purple-striped T-shirt. It was Paul. He was unattended; what if he couldn't find me and wandered off? The strain of responsibility immediately returned, elbowing out my earlier feelings of distant enjoyment of his quaintness. And it was then I realized I had lost some of the wonder of motherhood myself. Frazzled had replaced fun-loving, pressured had undermined precious. I determined to set aside the feelings of stress and enjoy my fascinating little boy.

Chapter 3 – Breaking the News

October 6

Phoning each of our children with the news was our next dreadful duty. Sunrise had never taken so long. We started with the ones who lived two hours ahead of our time zone. How painful it was to hear their cheerful answer to the ring knowing the terrible news we would have to give them. How cruel it felt to hold the power to ruin their day, change their life forever. Their disbelief, their anguish, the unanswerable question – "Why Paul?" – each response gripped our hearts tighter in a vice of pain.

Did God experience this pain as he watched the police drive up that morning while we slept, knowing our lives were about to be changed forever?

When our youngest, Timothy, 15, got up that morning, we had to explain to him the death of his brother. Timo's disability keeps him focused on the immediate. He loves simple pleasures and routine. We were uncertain how much he would understand. But we knew he loved and missed his siblings who'd left home. In tears, Mike described the early morning visit from the police and the news that Paul was now gone. Timothy broke into silent tears in his dad's arms. It is a rare thing for Timo to cry. He fights tears even when he's seriously provoked or injured. Was this weeping now a response to the even rarer sight of seeing his father in tears?

There were others to call too. I was surprised when my brother-in-law set up a conference call with my out-of-town sister rather than simply passing on the message to her. I was surprised too, when our pastor said he would come to be with us as soon as he could. Like a mountain climber in a mist, groping for a foothold and unaware of how far the summit is, the magnitude of what had happened had yet to dawn on me. Somehow, I had the uncomfortable idea that the more people who knew, the more certain was the truth. None of my reactions made sense but shock plays odd tricks with the mind. "Abnormal reactions to abnormal situations is normal behavior," Viktor Frankl observed of his fellow concentration camp prisoners.

Later that morning, we wondered if we should announce Paul's death on Facebook It seemed almost sacrilegious to give such news on a medium devoted to the flippant and foolish. Word of someone's death should be given in person, shouldn't it? But we were neither able nor inclined to make phone calls to everyone who needed to hear the news.

A near neighbor drove up just then. Gail chattered cheerfully, explaining why our phone lines were now dead. (We hadn't realized they were. Our earlier calls to family had worked fine.) Since recent roadwork, she told us, the local lines had been dug up and draped along several miles of barbed-wire fence. But that morning, an area farmer cultivating his field had snagged the line, causing a break in service. I stared into her perpetually smiling face as she chatted, wondering whether to tell her our news. I dreaded the awkwardness of facing someone who wouldn't know what to say. There *was* nothing to say. When I did tell her, I could see it didn't sink in. Her dazed look reflected the expression my own face must have worn when the police were at the door.

Once she left, Mike called the phone company on his cell phone to explain our urgent need to repair the phone lines, despite its being a holiday weekend.

"A death in the family," he explained. The words made my stomach clench. I wished he wouldn't say them to strangers. As for informing those outside the family via Facebook, we decided people may have had such reservations about the telephone when it was a new invention. Since social media is a means of communication, we used it to let people know.

That afternoon, we had our first opportunity to exercise grace to those who had a different way of expressing grief. Paul's grandmother, my mother-in-law arrived, greatly agitated. She was struggling with the callousness of whoever had driven the vehicle that struck and killed Paul. How could anyone do such a thing? What kind of person just leaves someone on the road to die? Maybe if they'd called an ambulance, Paul would still be alive!

Although I had prepared myself for people's awkward attempts at comfort I was unprepared for this kind of focus on the gruesome incident itself. My brain refused to think about the actual event. In my hazy state, I recognized that Paul's sufferings were over and it served no purpose to relive those moments.

I felt I should be a support and comfort to her, that I should at least sit down and talk with her, but I was simply unable. In a fog, I just kept plodding along with my halting preparations for the next day's Thanksgiving dinner. Chop onions and celery. Cut bread into chunks for stuffing. Peel potatoes. When she left after only a short stay, I felt guilty, watching her go and knowing she, too, was trying to fathom the unfathomable. Later we learned she went home and wrote a passionate letter to the city's newspaper editor expressing her outrage at the perpetrator of the crime. It seems she had misunderstood the circumstances and for months laboured under the impression the collision was intentional.

So, Mike, Timothy and I spent the rest of that day alone. It was as though life was in freeze-frame. Suspended in time, we went about a few chores, silent and pondering. My husband told me he'd knelt in the dry autumn grass beside Snickers, our younger dog, and wept into her auburn fur. She had been Paul's, brought to him as a puppy. Because she was his, she'd been spared a bullet for having run to their deaths three lambs he bought as an investment. Now she had outlived him.

That afternoon, lyrics to a song I didn't know well and hadn't heard for years ran through my mind continually. The fragment reminded me the Lord makes no mistakes, that he knows every detail of the path of my life.

My thoughts strained to remember the rest of it. As though I were clutching a tenuous lifeline to ultimate reality and trust in God, I hummed the lines again and again. Those few simple lines encapsulated for me the overwhelming message of scripture, that God is sovereign. But in that time of crisis that's all that came to mind.

I had little appetite and no ideas or initiative to make supper that evening. In silence, we drove the half-hour to town for pizza, hoping for anonymity. The friendly waitress knew us – her son had been on the same hockey team as Paul. But we said nothing about him. Speaking the words only seemed to hammer down the truth, making it truer. And making it worse.

Turning in the driveway on our return, I scanned the wide, flat expanse of acreage lawn that had been Paul's job to mow. Who would cut the grass next summer? I thought of his loud singing while riding the lawn tractor. He hadn't been amused when earlier in the season I teased him a little about the volume of his singing, but I recalled my pleasure at seeing him enjoy himself. It was the first positive memory to enter my mind since we'd heard the distressing news.

For the first time ever on that very long, very slow day, my tears began to flow.

Chapter 4 – Groping for Hope

October 7

Sunday morning dawned sunny and mild and we went to church as usual. I clung to the normalcy of our weekly practice, but the horrified expressions of people we met told me there was nothing normal about this Sunday. Apparently, word had gotten around because several people responded to us with hugs and words of sympathy. The escape from brutal reality I'd hoped to find there eluded me. I remember nothing of that Thanksgiving service but the condolences of the people.

The boys would be arriving in the afternoon for our planned Thanksgiving dinner so once we got home, I quickly threw together a soup-and-crackers lunch. News travels fast in our rural community. I was grateful others had done the calling so we hadn't had to reiterate the bad news over and over. But there was a sense in which I fought speaking the truth. Saying the words seemed to make it truer, more final.

We had barely finished eating when the first car drove in the yard. It was our near neighbours George and Rosanna. They are gentle Mennonites; kindness seeps from them. But part of me feared judgment. Perhaps if we'd been better parents we wouldn't be facing this sorrow and disgrace now. Perhaps if we had had a more extensive network of church family in the immediate vicinity, as our Mennonite neighbours did, Paul wouldn't have been so susceptible to the pull of the punk world.

Standing at the front door, we explained to our friends the little we knew about the circumstances surrounding Paul's death. For the first time I experienced the full impact of the horror.

My boy had lain, injured and dying, alone on a city street!

Rosanna looked at me without judgment. With sympathetic tears in her eyes, she squeezed my arm. "We are never alone," she reminded me. "'Though I walk through the valley of the shadow of death, Thou art with me.'" As I gazed into her compassionate face, this ancient promise settled into my soul with a brief ray of comforting hope.

Then she told me a story. Her twenty-two-year-old nephew had suffered a brain injury in a farm accident three years earlier. I knew this, and along with many others in our community, had prayed for his recovery during the three months he spent in a coma following the accident. What was new to me was that for the first time recently, Randy had been able to haltingly express bits of what he'd experienced while unconscious.

Just that week, Rosanna told me, he'd said he wished he could die. Troubled, they asked him why. Was it because life was now so hard for him? He said no. It was the wonder of the angels he had seen (while he was in a coma); they had been with him all that time, he said.

Here was something to ponder. Someone who had been unconscious for months, on the brink between life and death, was describing a state of awareness of the supernatural he experienced during that period. To observers, he had seemed entirely unresponsive yet he was aware of, and actively living a life unknown to the rest of us. Remembering something so tantalizingly sweet that lay beyond this world filled him with a longing to return.

I saw this as an opening to the possibility that there is awareness in unconsciousness. To me, it gave hope that while Paul's brain may have been badly injured, his spirit still could have been aware and responsive. And maybe, just maybe there had been moments. Moments to respond to God's love. Moments to respond to God's mercy. Moments for the heart to lurch to a stop in its headlong rush toward self-gratification and make that critical U-turn toward God.

More carloads of neighbours from the surrounding farms and ranches soon arrived, some well-known to us, some only acquaintances. Gradually our house filled up and, operating on such a mechanical setting as I was, I didn't even think to make coffee. I felt neglectful that I couldn't greet each one. It still hadn't occurred to me that the normal rules of socializing could be set aside under the circumstances.

Most of the visitors did not stay long. One couple who did, told the sad story of their sixteen-year-old grandson's death in a farm accident that summer. Mutual suffering forges a bond like little else can. This man commented that although he may have been known for having a temper, nothing had touched him more deeply than the loss of this boy. And nothing comforted him more than the hope that he would see his grandson in heaven someday. How significant, I thought, that brushes with death make us examine our lives. There's an unavoidable link between how we live our lives and our readiness to meet our Maker.

By supper time, I was so grateful to see three of our sons arrive. Most of the guests had already gone but we asked our pastor and his wife to stay for the meal. Our family offered them fleeting images and inconsequential memories of Paul as they came to mind. Later, we talked with the pastor and his wife alone about what had happened. I expressed some of my angst at the state of Paul's soul and my fear that he hadn't had enough time to repent.

"How long does it take?" Pastor Ross asked. He was right, of course. As my husband and I had discussed upon first learning of Paul's death, the time required to think, "I've been wrong! Forgive me Lord!" is only a twinkling.

We walk a tightrope in declaring that repentance can be done the split second before we die. On one side is the danger our hearers will put off that essential decision, with the risk of never making it. On the other side, if we insist that only a public profession of faith and a life lived consistent with that are indications of a person's eternal destiny, we run into the peril of thinking heaven is earned by what we say or do.

"The Bible, which ranges over a period of four thousand years, records but one instance of a deathbed conversion (the penitent thief), – *one* that none may despair, and *but* one that none may presume," wrote Puritan, William Guthrie.

Years earlier, I had studied the account of the thief crucified next to Jesus. Before I looked at it carefully, it seemed merely incidental, a simple aside. But I learned there were profound depths of truth inherent in it.

> *"There were also two others, criminals, led with Him to be put to death. And when they had come to the place called Calvary, there they crucified Him and the criminals, one on the right hand and the other on the left…*

Then one of the criminals who were hanged blasphemed Him, saying, 'If You are the Christ, save Yourself and us." But the other, answering, rebuked him, saying, 'Do you not even fear God, seeing you are under the same condemnation? And we indeed justly, receive the due reward of our deeds; but this Man has done nothing wrong.' Then he said to Jesus, 'Lord, remember me when You come into Your kingdom.' And Jesus said to him, 'Assuredly, I say to you, today you will be with Me in Paradise.'" (Luke 23:32-34; 39-43)

Now those truths became a foothold for hope. From those four brief verses only found in Luke's gospel, I learned there are no coincidences. All the wrong choices and intentional evil this man had done led him to an ultimate confrontation with his soul's maker, nailed right next to him. If God brought that criminal to the precise time and place where he would meet Jesus, surely he engineers all encounters. And if he does, then might he have brought the driver of the vehicle and my son together with split second timing for the express purpose of creating an encounter between Paul and his maker?

Like the criminal pinned to a cross, Paul, lying injured and abandoned on a city street, was utterly unable to *do* anything good in order to be accepted by God. No good deeds, no special ritual, no clever choice. Both the thief and Paul required an act of God to change them. Confronted with the majesty of Jesus, Paul's attention would have been undivided. A person's decision to place trust in Jesus is the final act in something that God set in motion long before then.

The thief next to Christ may have lived a sinful, selfish life, but his dying conversion and testimony lives on. It gives hope to the hopeless. Perhaps something good could still come of Paul's life.

God can even make use of what he opposes to achieve his good purposes. If an ancient criminal's sin couldn't stop almighty God from rescuing someone he had set his love upon, what made me think a modern young man's rebellion was an insurmountable barrier for an all-powerful God?

My problem was, *I wanted to know for certain.* And it was that essential, audible profession of faith from Paul that was so tragically missing.

A few weeks after the funeral, I was explaining to someone the pain I carried that of all our children, Paul was the only one I had never heard express faith.

"Aren't you glad it doesn't take that?" she asked me. I wasn't sure at first what she meant. It doesn't take a profession of faith? Or it doesn't take a verbal profession? Perhaps she was merely offering a glib platitude. But considering it further, I found her question to be profoundly true.

My urge to know for certain meant I was insisting that definite, specific words were used, *in my hearing.* Yet we do not and cannot know all that goes through another person's mind – either the fleeting thoughts or the profound, life-altering ones.

But that recognition came later. For the present, on that Sunday when death was still impossible and unreal, foreign and unfamiliar, my mind remained mired in the bog of despair.

Chapter 5 – Letter from Vicky

That evening with our pastor, he relayed a comment from Paul's former Sunday School teacher. The man had been impressed at how well Paul knew his Bible. *Right. The Bible he refused to read with me anymore last spring!* To me it was futile praise.

There had already been many people saying how nice our son was, how friendly, how kind and helpful. "He was a good kid," one of his friends from youth group had said. "Always smiling," another had told me. *Really?* I had trouble reconciling these comments with the recent images that sprang to my mind: His grudging and minimal efforts when asked to do chores around home, his unsmiling lack of response when I'd try to lighten the mood with a witty comment.

"I guess he saved his bad behavior for home," I said, hating the bitterness that tinged my words.

I described some of the troubling times we'd had with Paul in the years previous. In addition to the pastor's reminder that a change of heart can be the work of an instant, he said that from personal experience and years of counseling the bereaved, he'd learned a vital thing about grief.

"You're thinking about some of the bad memories of the last couple of years. But you had sixteen good years with your son. As time goes by, those sixteen years of memories will begin to outweigh the bad."

As hard as that was to imagine at the time, hope flickered through me at his words. In time, I was to see the truth of them.

Early that morning, I had already made a beginning on a eulogy in preparation for the funeral. I read it to the pastor and my husband for their approval. In it, I'd poured out my anguish over the poor choices Paul had been making and the serious consequences of his selfish pursuits. Life-shattering consequences not just for him, but now for those who loved him. Although I tried to hold back anger and vindictiveness, it must have spattered onto the page. I had written some of what I would have liked to say to Paul if I could. I wanted to shake him up, and other kids like him, to see the misery he'd caused. I was still in parenting mode. Still trying to make a rebellious young man think about his actions.

When I finished and looked up, there was a slight pause. Mike and the pastor exchanged glances. It was just too harsh, they told me. To my mind at that time, it was the unvarnished truth. I knew the old dictum, "Never speak ill of the dead." But my sore heart was hurting with turmoil and confusion. Irrational as it may sound, I felt Paul's death was just one more act of rebellion and spite on his part. I've always hated pretense and I felt it would be false to write glowing accounts about what a wonderful individual Paul was. Yet here were two men I deeply respected both cautioning me. I tore up the draft and later rewrote it.

Before the pastor and his wife left that evening, they gave us a hand-written letter from a woman from our church whom I didn't know. It was her son, a friend of Paul's from youth group, who'd made a point that morning after church to tell me Paul was a good kid. I read her letter the following day.

Eleanor:

I was deeply saddened to hear about Paul this morning. I didn't know Paul well but I had the privilege of visiting with him once when I drove a few youths to the [home of another church family] for a youth event [mid-December 2011]. During that visit, I learned that Paul loved music, particularly "punk," loved playing in a band, and seemed amused to tell me that he considered himself an anarchist. I confessed that I knew nothing about punk music so maybe he could start a "Christian punk" band. There was a bit of an awkward pause (he was probably planning ahead for a different ride home), after which he said, "I don't think so." Because I didn't know who he was, I asked Paul if he was a Christian. He said "Yes," so I tried to emphasize that it might be cool to be a Christian punk band. He laughed diplomatically and told me that that probably wouldn't happen.

There was more small talk (that I don't remember) but the reason I'm telling you this is because I thought you might like to know that Paul was comfortable telling a stranger that he was a Christian. I hope that brings you some comfort when you think about him.

She closed with expressions of sympathy and support for us on behalf of her and her family.

Here at last was something. But what? That business of being an anarchist was embarrassing. I recalled the back-and-forth email conversation my husband had had with Paul a couple of years earlier when the idea of anarchy had first come up. Although Mike's written approach was successful in getting a response from Paul, reason and logic made no impact on him. I retold my grandfather's frightful, first-hand accounts of having lived under anarchy's reign in the aftermath of the Bolshevik revolution when hunger and bandits roamed rural Russia. Nothing could sway Paul. In retrospect, I understand he hadn't thought the matter through but simply as a matter of identity, latched onto whatever the punk world was spouting.

But saying he was a Christian – what did it mean? Did he actually make a public declaration of belief in Jesus? There were, after all, several of his peers in the vehicle. Or was he merely going along to get along with the crowd he happened to be with? Was it mere reflex, having grown up in a Christian home? And yet, when Paul applied to go on a summer mission trip with a church youth group at sixteen, he was candid about his uncertainties. "I have grown up in a Christian home. I have been taught that there is a God, that Jesus is his Son, that the Bible is his Word to humans, but I'm not sure right now where I stand."

The conversation described in the letter had taken place when Paul was seventeen, almost a year previous. What were we to make of the things that happened in the months following – in spring when he told me he didn't want to read the Bible with me anymore? Or the following summer only weeks before he left home, when he refused to attend church with us?

Dangling in that haze of unreality in the early days, assailed by jagged fears, I bumped repeatedly against what was both comforting and terrifying. *There's no one to cling to but God!* When Jesus had finished giving some hard teaching to his disciples, many of them gave up following him. What he taught didn't make sense to them. Jesus turned to his closest friends and asked if they, too, would leave. "Lord, to whom shall we go? You have the words of eternal life," Peter answered. (John 6:68) But the words of eternal life carried with them conditions and it was those conditions of repentance and belief that, in Paul's case, tormented me. Round and round my thoughts swirled, always eventually finding solidity in Psalm 73. "Whom have I in heaven but You? And there is none upon earth that I desire besides You. My flesh and my heart fail; But God is the strength of my heart and my portion forever." (73:25, 26)

Chapter 6 – Ashamed of my Son

I had sensed something changing in Paul for some time. In August 2009, when he was fifteen, in order to make a high school educational plan, I'd asked him what kind of career path he'd like to shoot for.

"I think I'd like to be an architect," he told me. I was pleased. It would mean hard work through high school and plenty of money toward education, yet it was something he was well suited to and for which I thought he clearly had the aptitude. So, we signed him up for on-line schooling for his core academic courses to gain accreditation. But it was like pulling teeth. I had to be after him to get assignments done and check them over, often having to insist he make revisions because of his half-hearted effort. In those years, I was plagued by a recurring nightmare, a throw-back to my own college days, that reflected the stress his behaviour was causing me: A thirty-page paper is due the next day and I haven't started yet. Or, I discover a few days before graduation that a certain course is required, yet I have never gone to classes.

My husband advised we should let Paul experience failure. My fear was that with his future at stake, he was not mature enough to make the right choice, leading to long-term negative consequences. Eventually, after two years' slogging, Paul said he was ready to give it up. And what was it he wanted to do with his life?

"Play in a punk band."

That hurt. The thought of my precious son throwing away his God-given talents was the emotional equivalent of tossing a priceless painting into a fire.

I was no stranger to punk rock culture. As far back as my college days in the early 80s, I'd had classmates who were fans of the music and dressed the part. I understood the culture to have grown out of the feelings of alienation and disenfranchisement experienced by young people, first in England, then spreading elsewhere. "England's punk scene had political and economic roots," an on-line history of punk explains. "The economy in the United Kingdom was in poor shape, and unemployment rates were at an all-time high. England's youth were angry, rebellious and out of work. They had strong opinions and a lot of free time," according to one historian of punk.

"'Punk Rock' was originally used to describe the garage musicians of the '60's. Bands like the Sonics were starting up and playing out with no musical or vocal instruction, and often limited skill. Because they didn't know the rules of music, they were able to break the rules… [Punk bands] were producing music that often bordered on noise. They were expanding the definitions of music without even realizing it."

Early punk rock dealt with social issues like oppression of the lower classes, the threat of a nuclear war, unemployment, or personal problems like depression. The genre, overall, expressed a subversive, rebellious anger. Lyrics railed against the establishment, injustice, cruelty and other social ills. But besides visceral screaming, no solutions to these problems ever seemed to be offered. What was the point of the music and the dressing up?

Were the costumes and culture merely a sales gimmick? Was today's punk anger now directed at protesting social evils like war, racism or homelessness? The effect was the same as it used to be. I couldn't see how punk music and culture offered any constructive solutions to social problems. Just a blast of violent anger. The inherent message was rejection of everything we stood for.

I had always viewed the young people enmeshed in the punk scene as lost children whose families hadn't provided them with the stability, guidance, boundaries and love to help them find purpose in life and resist peer influence. In the years of raising our family, whenever I'd see punks on city streets, my first thought would be sorrow for the home life that had prompted such anger and need for attention. Their despair drove them to seek notice any way they could get it and they were in desperate need of God's love. But another feeling, too, would follow the pity: compassion for confused and hurting kids.

Now I watched with growing apprehension as Paul became increasingly intrigued with the genre his brothers had introduced to him. I knew it was attractive to the suppressed and the voiceless, but I couldn't understand what possible appeal it could have to those who'd grown up in stable, loving environments. To find my own sons attracted to the punk subculture amounted, I felt, to a big fat F on my parenting report card.

Glancing through a book on punk's history that Paul had ordered through our local library, I noticed a pattern. At least by their own account, the musicians all seemed to come from dysfunctional homes.

"Do you relate to these people's background?" I asked him once, half afraid of his response.

"Not really," he said. Well, that was something at least.

Years later, his brother tried to explain the pull of the punk world. "It was mostly to do with being drawn to the opposite of what you've grown up with."

That overarching theme of rebellion, however, became more and more disturbing as I watched it appear on his doodling, his guitar, T-shirts he designed for himself and a thrift store leather jacket he covered in studs and patches. These all carried slogans that were the antithesis of every value we'd tried to instill in our children.

"Young, Poor and Angry!"

"Anarchy!"

"Bloody Hells."

"Crass."

"Don't Ask for Permission."

And the images! Punk seemed to have a dark obsession with death and decay, hatred, anger and the obscene. Skulls and skeletons abounded. In fact, one of the many punk subgenres was called "crust punk," something Paul seemed to especially enjoy. In his room, I found a meticulously drawn card he'd made for his girlfriend; two skulls with mohawks, cheekbone to cheekbone, entitled "Crust Love." Slashing fonts and harsh colours matched the angry sound that I found depressing and frightening on the rare occasions I heard what he was listening to. It hurt to see a new patch on his jacket carrying the slogan, "Against All Authority." We had taught our children to respect and obey authority, first God's, then human authority. How could I not take this personally and interpret it as a glimpse into the attitude of his own heart? I had avoided listening to the punk songs Paul and his brothers shared online; it truly seemed mere noise, but it was a ferocious noise that made my heart lurch. It was an enemy stealing my children from me and I was helpless to defend them because they went willingly.

Whether our son intended it or not, these images and messages were an assault. Clearly, the punk movement meant them that way. The punk method of countering the culture was to shock and attack. There was an overwhelming anger and violence to the imagery. Again, it was the opposite of what Christianity offers – love, joy, peace, forgiveness, new life.

I knew that God looks at the hearts of people and that wisdom meant seeing as God sees. Thirty years earlier in my college student center, a Christian drama group offered a unique take on Jesus' parable of the Good Samaritan. They depicted the social pariah Samaritan as a punk rocker who unexpectedly had compassion on a battered and beaten wayfarer. The message was lasting: judging by outward appearance alone is always wrong.

For me, it had been one thing to show love to punks in college. It was an entirely different matter to have my own children transforming themselves into something unrecognizable. I fought feelings of shame and embarrassment when Paul would insist on being seen in public in full regalia.

Now as we pondered the recent years of Paul's life, a magazine ad I'd once seen resonated with me. It featured a youth dressed in full punk attire – studded leather, safety pins, tattoos, piercings, garish-coloured mohawk. Beneath that was the slogan:

You gave up on having the perfect kid. At least you can have the perfect car.

Obviously, I wasn't the only one whose dreams for my children didn't include that get-up and the attitudes that went with it.

Chapter 7 – Hit and Run

Inexplicably, we were sleeping soundly each night. In fact, I looked forward to bed-time as an escape. The problem was the daily awakening. I'd lie there feeling well-rested and comfortable until I'd think, "Oh yeah. *That.*" And the fog of unreality would descend again. It was not a mist that crept lightly, softening the outlines of a harsh reality. Instead, it obliterated all other concerns; from our renovations planned for the following week, to international news of the Benghazi debacle. The fog spread its weighty, dark oppression over me, crushing down on my chest. Sleep became a welcome reprieve from the relentless treadmill of questions cycling through my mind throughout the day. *What actually happened that night? Had Paul been foolishly out on the road, drunk and careless?*

Unanswered questions swirled about the events of that Friday night. The police were keeping us informed as they made progress in the case but rumours via Facebook and the punk crowd had been flying. A taxi driver had come forward, claiming to be a witness to the accident. No, this rumour later proved false. Paul was found on the bridge by a passerby. Then we heard he'd been found on the grass at the end of the bridge. Maybe someone had dragged him there. Or maybe he was walking on the grass when hit? My hope-hungry heart latched onto this explanation. It indicated the driver must have been off the road, seriously drunk and therefore it absolved Paul of blame in the incident. The temptation was powerful to find a narrative, any rationalization at all, that someone other than my boy was to blame for his death. I was already bereft, my beloved son torn from me. To add to the pain by placing blame back on him was unbearable!

However, the next word we had from police was that he was, in fact, found in the middle of the left-hand lane. *Why wasn't he on the sidewalk? Was he drunk, and if so, was Paul himself at fault?*

By Saturday evening, we had learned the vehicle that hit Paul had been found. Sunday evening, the driver of the vehicle turned himself in to police. Tuesday's Red Deer Advocate carried a front-page article on the incident.

Man found dead on bridge

DRIVER HUNTED AFTER HIT-AND-RUN FATALITY SATURDAY

Red Deer RCMP are looking for a hit-and-run driver after a man was found lying fatally injured on Taylor Drive bridge early Saturday.

Police say the man was found about 2:05 a.m. lying in the northbound lanes on the bridge. He had been fatally injured after being struck by a car, said police.

"The suspect vehicle and driver did not remain at the scene of the collision and evidence at the scene indicated that the vehicle has sustained significant front-end damage," says a release [from police].

...The teen, who sported a green mohawk, and played guitar and piano, was well liked by all, [a family member] said.

Seeing our son's picture on the front page of the paper and the headline's use of the word "man" set off a battlefield of emotion within me. *Man? He was just a boy! My boy! It remained to be seen what kind of man he would become, and now we'll never know!*

I was grateful the photo was not a recent one but rather, a shot obtained from Facebook taken three years before where he looked quite normal. Still, the fact that our boy was out roaming the streets in the wee hours of the morning "sporting" an outlandish hair-do filled me with profound shame. And now this bit of teenage foolishness was published for all to read. My feelings of disgrace revealed something nasty about me. I assumed anyone's response would be what mine had often been on hearing news like this.

"What was the kid doing on the bridge at that hour? Probably drunk." After all, bad things are bound to happen to people that are out when and where they shouldn't be, right? I know these are not thoughts unique to me. On-line comments responding to tragic deaths freely blame and condemn the victim and his parents. When we can pinpoint the cause of a tragedy, we've found a way to ensure we won't experience it ourselves.

In fact, in those early weeks, I received a phone call from a relative asking questions along those lines. My heart slumped as I admitted I had no answers. We had tried to keep Paul safe, to train him up in the way he should go as the Bible instructs, but we had failed. Underlying the blame game revealed by these sorts of responses was the darker sentiment that he got what he deserved. In my mind, the news article reader's question was bound to lead to, "Why can't parents keep their kids under control?" To uproot those gut responses would take many months and much grieving.

Most of all, it would take the full force of biblical truth about what we all deserve and the meaning of grace.

By the following day, our local town paper had reported that police had found the suspect vehicle and arrested a 24-year-old Red Deer man.

"[He] was charged with failing to stop and render assistance at the scene of a collision and for public mischief," [police] said. Quoting a police officer, the article continued, "Investigation has revealed that there was a passenger in the suspect vehicle at the time of the collision…" The RCMP were urging "that passenger to contact the lead investigator … immediately."

My mind reached out to the parents of the young man at fault in Paul's death – their angst over their son's future and beneath that their inevitable pain at the cold, hard, immutable fact of his having caused a death. If I could feel compassion for them and their son, why did I assume readers of the news held an attitude of judgment toward us? Might they not also feel compassion?

Soon we were informed the accused had opted to be tried by a judge alone. The prosecutor said juries are usually strongly biased against impaired drivers who cause the death of a person, which may have influenced the young man's decision.

Later in the week, the police officer who had attended the scene of the collision, called to ask for information. I took the opportunity to ask him some questions. He explained Paul had been found in the middle of the road, lying parallel to the driving lane. The officer said EMS had arrived seconds after he, himself had and, although there had been "some respiration," they pronounced our son dead almost immediately. He added that there was surprisingly little blood at the scene. I felt desperate to know if the first person on the scene had heard Paul say anything. Perhaps he whispered the name of Jesus? How precious it would have been to learn he murmured words he'd memorized years before from II Timothy, "I know whom I have believed…"

"No," the officer answered, sounding regretful. There had been no words. Paul had not been conscious. My hope that he may have said something, perhaps expressed faith in some way, evaporated.

Chapter 8 – What Really Happened?

Slowly, in a process that is still not complete and may never be, we began to piece together the last day and hours of Paul's life. With explanations and memories from those who were with him, from on-location visits, and a bit of guesswork, I've retraced Paul's steps on what was to be his final day on earth.

In the lovely fall weather that day, he and his brother had stretched wire and hammered staples, erecting a rural page-wire fence, two hours east of town. But Paul was beyond excited anticipating the evening. He and Jonny left work early so Paul could get to the music store by four p.m. He needed to pick up the new amp for his guitar in time for their band, Red City Drunk Punx (R.C.D.P.), to play downtown that night. On that long two-hour drive home, he listened carefully to Evacuate's song, "This Night is Ours." And that night would be theirs! By the time they got home, Paul had memorized it enough to play it himself. But what he was most looking forward to was the thrill of having the band play, for the first time ever, a song he'd written.

He must have felt so free – no disapproving parents over his shoulder, no schoolwork deadlines, no chores to do. Moving into town with his brothers had long been a dream of his. "I've gotta move out," he'd often told his brothers on the few weekends he'd been allowed to spend with them since they'd left home. It had been only six weeks since he'd joined them and he had yet to pay rent, but he regularly chipped in for groceries. There were certain foods he'd hanker for and doing the cooking himself was a way to ensure he'd get them.

One damper on his spirits was a recent call from Samantha (not her real name), his girlfriend of a year and a half. A couple of weeks earlier, she had broken up with him because, since he'd moved into Red Deer, they saw each other so infrequently. Perhaps Paul blamed his parents for this; they certainly had not made things easy for him to spend time with her. But there were other girls in town. One, in particular, had caught his eye and he was looking forward to seeing her that evening. He took extra care with his mohawk that night, pleased with the nice bright neon green he'd been able to achieve once he'd figured out the right product and method. His earlier attempt had resulted in the sickly grey-green colour of sun-bleached seaweed. Tonight too, he'd be sporting the new studded dog collar that had recently come in the mail. He shrugged on his black leather jacket, glittering with another section of painstakingly applied spikes, and he was set.

Slumland, the downtown, all-ages music venue where bands of various genres offered their music to local fans, pulsed with energy. It was about the size of a large home rec room. In the low-lit windowless basement, two walls were painted black. One side of its blue rear wall was painted with a large zombie girl, while at the other, a bar served alcohol, soft drinks, candy and chips. Punks didn't buy hard liquor so the drink of choice that night was beer.

Opposite the bar a low stage, brightly lit and bristling with sound equipment, was backed by a black wall splashed with the green and white tag of a graffiti artist.

There was an eager, carefree atmosphere as young people started to arrive in twos and threes. For one evening a month, the punk community offered a flipped-bird salute to the demands of the teachers, employers, bureaucrats or customers of their daily lives. Girls and guys were decked out in eye-catching get-up – torn stockings worn with high-top runners, spiked hair in a rainbow of colours, leather or denim jackets covered in studs of all sizes and lengths. Across the black-and-white tiled floor, groups of kids gave casual greetings or hugs to familiar faces in the tight-knit scene.

Paul felt at home, in his element. This is where he wanted to be; where he'd dreamed of being each weekend for the last two years instead of stuck at home watching parent-approved movies or at another tame church youth event. At last he could be himself! Now that he was eighteen, he could freely order anything he wanted at the bar, too.

Waiting for the girl who'd waved at him across a campfire recently, Paul headed to the bar with the others and ordered a beer. But the adrenaline rush of the atmosphere of anticipation was almost potent enough. He finally spotted the girl and made his way over to her. He never really knew how to start a conversation with a girl, with anyone for that matter. But a grin or a goofy face seemed to break the ice most of the time. That night Wave Girl did most of the talking. Apparently, all she'd been doing the other night at the campfire was waving smoke away from her face, which explained her big smile when he waved back. Embarrassing. But it seemed to amuse her, which led to further conversation between them.

The venue's manager remembers Paul goofing around and laughing in the lobby that night. He knocked a stack of fliers off her desk just to bug her, she said, "but he picked them up, too." Nervous excitement had him keyed up, anticipating their performance.

R.C.D.P. was the last of four bands scheduled to play that night. As the first band warmed up, the small crowd of twenty to thirty young people chafed to get moving. Then the air was split with an opening riff and the kids started jumping, bumping. As though on pogo sticks, girls and boys found the rhythm, breaking it only for a quick shoulder or hip bump with a laughing friend. The room began to heat up.

Sometime around 11:30, the third band finally cleared off the stage. It was time. The Drunk Punx hurried to set up, exchanging elated glances. *This night is ours!* Onstage, with Jonny on drums, Paul on electric guitar, and Joey on bass, lead singer Ryker made love to his mike in a blast of angry volume. Then came Paul's piece. Ripping his T-shirt off, he played the first notes of *Army of Chaos.* Over and over he'd practiced it at home, but without the amp lest his mom have a fit. Now with the other instruments and singers, and full amplification, he could finally let loose. And he gave it all he had. Though small in number, the crowd seemed to love it.

Army of Chaos

We're the … punx!
The rebels you will fear!
An army of insurgents,
Get out of our way.
*F--- you and your hippie sh*t*
Love gets you nowhere!
Peace is a delusion,
It's only veiled hate!
It's time to bring the chaos,

This is our common goal!
The revolution's coming,
Get … out of its way!

Chorus:
We're the army! The army of chaos!
The army! The army of chaos!
A riot's what we need,
*Get drunk and f--- sh*t up!*
A lighter and a 40oz will set this city ablaze!

And more lyrics that were never used in the song:

The few of us that stand against the status quo
We are the ones who fight for those who can't stand up for themselves!
A disease, a plague, a virus,
Call us what you will!
It won't be long before nobody cares what you say!

As the Drunk Punx finished their set, things began winding down in the Slumland venue. The band packed up their gear and the crowd thinned out. Wave Girl hung around while Paul stowed his guitar and unplugged his amp. It was after midnight when his brother Jonny finished covering his drum set and told Paul he was heading home.

Even though he was tired from playing so hard, Paul was not yet ready for the night to end. Glancing at the girl, he told Jonny, "I'll just walk home. Leave the door unlocked for me."

Still later, with only a handful of people left in the venue, another couple, Jake and Kristyn, offered Paul a ride home. But as long as he was with Wave Girl, he was good to walk. Finally, the two left Slumland and headed north from downtown.

The two of them walked up the street to the nearest convenience store where Paul decided he craved something sweet. Forget all the rules from the orthodontist! That night was a triumph to celebrate! He grabbed a favourite he hadn't had in a long time and definitely on the ortho-forbidden list – a Charleston Chew – and other munchies. At the checkout he had a sudden urge to cool his cheek on the counter, a move that may have raised the eyebrow of the store clerk but made Wave Girl giggle. She seemed to find him clever and funny. Heck, Paul was finding himself clever and funny. It was becoming clearer that the two of them might have a bit of a thing going. But walking home, all too soon the girl needed to turn off toward her place and Paul was on his own.

Welcoming the mild fall chill, his mind went over and over the events of the night without much thought about his route, a path he'd often walked since moving to Red Deer in August. With stores and businesses closed, walking the empty streets, Paul belted out his very own hit single as he liked to do when he was alone. Perhaps plans for other songs and dreams of future gigs filled his thoughts.

Nearing the four-lane Taylor Drive Bridge, Paul had a choice. Walking from the convenience store on the right side of the street, he would have approached the north-bound, right side of the bridge. Home was located straight ahead, also on the right side of Taylor Drive, at the first intersection beyond the far end of the bridge. Between the north- and south-bound sections of bridge edged by waist-high concrete barriers was a twelve-foot gap spanned by wide-spaced cable grid. The bridge's only sidewalk ran along the far left, south-bound lanes.

By now, an early morning's start at the physical labour of fencing, and the fading adrenaline rush of the evening made him simply want to get home to bed. Taking the sidewalk meant he'd have to cross four lanes to get to it, walk over the bridge, take the pedestrian overpass and backtrack down the right side of the street to reach home. With the streets deserted as they were, did he decide to take his chances, starting up the right-hand bridge? On that side, there are two lanes for traffic and a third, narrower lane on the right for emergency stops. Was he walking along that narrow lane when he was hit? At the crest of the bridge, he would have been able to see the streetlight in front of their duplex. Almost home.

And then – collision.

Chapter 9 – A Dropped Thread?

Are any of the choices we make in this life small or insignificant? Do minutes, seconds matter? If Paul had gone home with his brother or the young pair that offered him a ride, would he still be alive today? This is the point where what-ifs give way to if-onlys. How long does it take to walk across a driving lane? A minute? Thirty seconds? Five?

Does anything happen merely by chance?

Years earlier, on a family trip with Paul, we had listened to an audio-book, The Grand Weaver. In it, author Ravi Zacharias tells the story of a young American mid-westerner named Elgin Staples who served his ship in battle against a Japanese destroyer in August of 1944. Wounded in both legs when his ship suffered a direct hit that night, Staples was swept into the dark Pacific Ocean. Just in time, he managed to activate a narrow life belt. It kept him alive. Hours later, rescue by a passing cruiser restored him to his ship only to set him adrift again when the ship sank. Finally, many hours after that, he was picked up by a troop transport. Staples was one of only five hundred survivors. During the return voyage to the United

States, he found himself memorizing every detail of the precious belt that saved his life. It had been manufactured by the Firestone Tire & Rubber Company of Akron, Ohio and bore a registration number. Back home, he was reunited with his mother who had worked for Firestone during the war effort. His mother explained that Firestone had insisted on a high standard of quality control, assigning a unique number to each employee. When the young sailor recited to his mother the registration number of the belt that had saved his life, she stared at him, electrified.

"That was my personal code that I affixed to every item I was responsible for approving," she told him.

> *History is so replete with such "coincidences," one is pushed to conclude an Invisible Hand orchestrates the flow of its events. It was this invisible hand that I now clung to. Confluence is the flowing together, like two merging rivers, of sometimes widely divergent events at precisely the same time. Some suggest this confluence, so obvious in scripture, only applies to biblical history. But the interconnectedness of every event must mean nothing happens by chance. "The events of redemption that happen within the framework of ordinary history give us the deeper assurance that all of history is in His hands. It means the crisis moments in our own lives are not expressions of vanity or futility.*
>
> - Theologian R.C. Sproul in his book *The Invisible Hand*

There may be any number of coincidences we experience in a lifetime of which we're completely unaware. I myself experienced one near miss that only now do I see as significant. In 1981, a couple of weeks prior to my wedding, I was about to cross a city street when a right-turning car rounded the corner at the intersection directly in front of me. I was not struck but it missed me by mere inches. Floating in my own private world of bridal lace and wedding invitations, I thought little of the traffic event at the time. Mainly, I was perplexed at why the passenger in the vehicle was so fervent in asking me if I was alright. Now I wonder, why was Paul's life snuffed out in an instant while mine was not? Had I been one step further onto the intersection – a matter of moments – I could have been seriously injured or killed. If that had happened, my wedding would not have occurred and none of my children would have been born.

"God, who made the world and everything in it … has determined [mankind's] preappointed times and the boundaries of their dwellings…" (Acts 17:24, 26) Preappointed times carry a staggering tapestry of human choices, history and events. Thread after thread is interwoven and dependent upon all that has gone before. In the very conception of a child there are multiple threads and unfathomably long sequences of concurrence.

For Paul to be on the Red Deer Taylor Street Bridge in the early morning hours of October 6, 2012 required him to be born in 1994 so that he would be of age, freely walking the streets of Red Deer that night. In turn, it required me to be born, which might not have occurred if the child before me that my parents lost at five months' gestation had lived. My parents had to be born, meet at a boarding school in Manitoba and marry. Their parents had to meet and marry their spouses. All four of my grandparents had to survive the Bolshevik revolution and famine in Russia, which required my teenaged grandmother's hiding place in the pig sty *not* to be discovered so that she was *not* raped and murdered by hostile bandits. My grandfather had to survive the gruesome and dangerous World War I battlefield where he served as medic. Add to this complex confluence, the unlikely odds that both sets of my grandparents immigrated to Canada in 1926, among the last wave of Mennonites to be allowed out of the country. The following year, none were permitted out of the country. A year later, another group of emigres arrived in Moscow only to be sent to Siberia when the Stalinist regime reneged on its agreement to allow them to leave.

And that's only the briefest details of merely three generations of just *one* side of Paul's heritage. Pile onto these the complexity of choices and circumstances that put the driver of the vehicle in the exact place and the precise moment of the collision between car and pedestrian and the contingencies are mind-boggling.

No. Chance is not an adequate answer to the question of why something happens. From a human perspective, the collision that took Paul's life was an accident. From a divine view, there was a perfectly planned purpose in it. I simply couldn't imagine what it was.

Chapter 10 – More and More Questions

One particularly sharp pain for me was the lack of anything to be proud of in Paul's recent life.

It was Monday, October 8; Thanksgiving Day. I was on Facebook, checking the Remembering Paul page our nephew had created, reading and appreciating the many condolences written there. Somehow, I came across a recent funeral for a teen-aged young man I didn't know. The memorial slide show revealed a boy who eagerly gave his time to serving others. It seemed, in fact, that he'd died while on a mission trip. His mother gave a glowing eulogy of how her son had loved God and people and in turn, had been loved by many.

Through the years, I'd heard of tragically-killed teens who made an impact for God on this world, disproportionate to their short life. One of the more famous ones was Cassie Bernall, murdered while praying as she hid from the killers in Columbine High School in April 1999. And there were many others. Here's what someone wrote on Facebook in 2015 about one such boy:

> *We can draw comfort, knowing that 13-year-old Patrick is with our Lord, as he had professed faith and become a Christian earlier this year. Patrick has been a blessing to those who have gotten to know him with his gentle spirit and willingness to help... His father shared how Patrick would witness to him about what he was learning through the Bible. The family shared how Patrick had changed for the better and how he was happiest when he was at church helping and being in fellowship.*

Paul, on the other hand, was not killed while on a mission trip helping the poor; he did not die a soldier's death fighting for freedom for the oppressed. He had not lived a life of selfless service nor did he die a martyr's death, standing up for truth. He died while pursuing his own personal happiness. Yes, I knew he could as easily have been killed walking home from a church youth event or on a simple shopping trip. But that wasn't the case. We were left with soured memories of the recent past and a death that gave us no comfort that something good might come of it. It seemed his suffering and ours was a meaningless waste.

In his book *Man's Search for Meaning,* psychiatrist Viktor Frankl states that suffering in life is inevitable. But, he emphasizes, it is vitally important to find meaning and purpose in it. "If there is a meaning in life at all, then there must be a meaning in suffering," he wrote. Similarly, we crave meaning and purpose in our death, its manner and its timing. My struggle was finding that elusive meaning in Paul's.

Just when I would despair, in those early days, of God's ability to bring anything good out of this tragedy, the refrain of the song constantly playing in my mind would return with added force: The Lord makes no mistakes."

Again and again, I returned to my one solace – the rock-solid belief that to God, what happened to Paul was not an accident.

"If I thought even for one moment that a single molecule were running loose in the universe outside the control and domain of Almighty God, I wouldn't sleep tonight," Sproul has written.

Psalm 121:4 tells us that God "who keeps you … shall neither slumber nor sleep." Nor is God ever surprised or disappointed. Because of this, I knew there had to be a purpose in the pain; there *had* to be meaning to it.

I knew the trials and sufferings of this life are *designed* to chase us to God. Everywhere I turned in those early days after the tragedy, I was reminded of that truth. A line from a poem by an unknown author I heard quoted that Monday described how we can even be grateful for the pressures and troubles of life because they refocus our hearts and minds on our Creator.

> *"Pressed into knowing no helper but God*
> *Pressed into loving the staff and the rod."*

Only the week before, I had sent my father a poem by Martha Snell Nicholson, hoping it would comfort him in his long-term disability:

The Thorn

I stood a mendicant of God before His royal throne
And begged him for one priceless gift which I could call my own.
I took the gift from out His hand, but as I would depart
I cried, "But Lord, this is a thorn and it has pierced my heart.
This is a strange, a hurtful gift which Thou hast given me."

He said, "My child, I give good gifts and gave My best to thee."

I took it home and though at first the cruel thorn hurt sore,

As long years passed I learned at last to love it more and more.

I learned He never gives a thorn without this added grace:

He takes the thorn to pin aside the veil which hides His face.

Now it was my turn to be given a thorn to pierce my heart. In vague, unfocused phrases, I prayed God would bring something good out of it.

Please Lord, don't let this incredible pain be for nothing!

Until I knew what that purpose was, however, what I'd learned in past seasons of pain and sorrow kept me tethered now. I knew I had Jesus to console me every step of the way. Almost tangibly, I sensed his immediate presence. I clung to scriptures that, years before, had leapt off the page and into my heart, becoming my very own.

"In all their affliction He was afflicted,
And the Angel of His Presence saved them;
In His love and in His pity He redeemed them;
And He bore them and carried them
All the days of old" (Isaiah 63:9).

To know the Maker of the universe feels my pain! To be carried by God! Without doubt, that was happening; I could sense it. Some say Christianity is a crutch. I found knowing Jesus to be much more than that. It was a wheelchair.

Chapter 11 – The Memory Box

In the haze of that week between Paul's death and his funeral, I had a moment of clarity. Our family had already paged through the photo albums weeping and remembering. Now I brought out Paul's memory box to see if it held any clues to his spiritual state. I pulled out the white copy-paper box with his name on it and we began to poke tentative fingers at the contents. On top was Paul's favourite, formerly-fuzzy white blanket, now a ragged gray-white screen with all its fuzz loved off and its satin binding in shreds. Tears welled up in my eyes as I remembered the little boy I'd snuggled in that blanket when both were fresh and new.

There was a little alphabet-print shirt my mother had sewn for Paul, worn thin from almost daily wear when he was four. Hockey trophies, 4-H horse club paperwork, school assignments and craft projects cluttered the box, but above all, drawings. We found hundreds of pages of drawings. The earliest, from about age six, were colourful diagrams of jewels and their various cuts which he'd copied from the encyclopedia. For the longest time we'd had no idea what he meant when he referred to a "lentil-shaped cabochon."

It was a French term he'd read strictly according to English phonetic rules. In the memory box, there were endless cataloged pages of real and imaginary medieval weaponry. There were lists too, in Paul's tight block-printing of whatever his current interest mania was at any given time. Most intriguing to us was the world he invented with maps and languages.

Paul had always had a way with words. On his own somehow, at about age three, he had learned to read and from there it was a short step to writing. One of his early efforts when he was six, was an ode to his precious blanket, always known as whiteblanket, or "my white". The accompanying illustration, "Whiteblanket," pencil on white paper, doesn't do justice to the much-loved source of comfort.

> *I've had my whiteblanket since I was a baby. When it comes out of the dryer it's warm and cozy. Most of the binding has been ripped off. Oh, ya and the fuzz is ripped off.*
>
> *I love my whiteblanket to sleep with, to hug and to squeeze and to make me feel better when I'm hurt.*

In that year's Christmas newsletter his oldest brother Ben described Paul as a voracious reader: "Some of his personal favourites are Tin Tin comic books and the Picture Bible. He also enjoys Calvin and Hobbes. One of his best loved strips is one in which Calvin, the six-year-old protagonist, immortalizes his most hideous facial expressions during class pictures. We witnessed impressive Calvinesque resemblances after this summer's family photos were developed."

At about age seven, Paul wrote to Ben, who may have been wishing for news from home. Paul had spent weeks poring over the encyclopedia, and copying down every listing of birds or animals –

a total of 484. He typed out the completed, alphabetized "Animal ABC," and sent it off to Ben without any personal details.

By the time Paul was nine, he spent his free time tackling lengthier pieces, with the kind of detail that only an insatiably hungry, growing boy could conceive.

> *One cold day after sledding for two hours, me and two of my friends, Chris and Felix, were at my house watching "The Mask of Zorro", and I was making peanut butter crackers, popcorn, juice, hot chocolate, apple cider, (the cookies were already made, same with the candy, fudge, marshmallows and nachos) and putting them on a platter. My mom ordered pizza, went to A&W to get hamburgers, hot dogs, whistle dogs, fries, pop, and more hamburgers. She made sloppy joes, Denver sandwiches, and bread and cheese all piled together to make sandwiches. The last thing to do was to make the onion rings. My mom had the A&W recipe for them too…*

In this fourteen-chapter story, the TV screen morphs into a real-life battle with enemy creatures coming out of the set and the boys enter a fantasy world. Scenes of intense action are broken by lengthy lists of the animals, trees and fruit indigenous to that world. Paul's tendency to catalogue and list things was unique among our children. What began with jewels, medieval weaponry and armour, expanded in later years to lists of every species of ape, hockey players and their statistics, and hockey cards he owned or hoped to get.

When he read *The Lord of the Rings* a new interest was born. He described his creative process in a 4-H speech. A map began to grow, requiring names in a foreign language, so words spelled backwards began a linguistic effort that led to a dictionary of increasingly lengthy words. "For example, if you wanted to say, "The doctor is in," you would have to say, "The doctor is jaralarinarazonfarzon." He spent hours planning and peopling his world, complete with its own bigotries and intrigues, dangers of nature and warfare.

In Grade 11, Paul had an online school writing assignment that he'd put off for far too long. One Friday morning, I gave him the ultimatum to get it done by noon or he would forfeit going to hockey practice later in the day. What he produced was a fairly accurate description of every high school assignment I ever had to nag him to complete.

> *Once upon a time there was a frustrated and uninspired kid who couldn't write a story for a school assignment. He tried and tried for days to think of something, anything. But it was not to be. All he could think about was Big Powerful Russians, and how cold it was in that drafty house, and how warm he could have potentially been if he could just get upstairs unnoticed, and then, oh! Those blankets! He put it off for about eight years, (or so it seemed) but still had no ideas. His brain simply would not turn on. The very thought of writing repulsed him, and he put it off further. By then, the problem had grown from small to hideous, which is not even on the Size Scale. He thought he had better tackle it before it grew beyond even the Ugly Scale, which as we all know, can lead to one of the most feared of the scales, the Incontinence Scale.*
>
> *So, he began to write. The first few feeble sentences he wrote were nothing less than the most disorganized he had written thus far in his career. But still he plugged on, writing a few words, then a few more. He would simply have to do it. Not tomorrow, not a little later, but right now. His story was very long and*

boring, being nothing more than an autobiography of his experiences at the writing desk, staring at an almost blank piece of paper for three and a half hours a night, and went on and on, very much like this sentence, in which he described every detail of the chipped Rich Walnut-stained desk, the slow, tedious work he had to put into each word, and the many hair-tearing, paper-shredding fits of fury at the monotony of his work. But the story slowly began to grow, despite the many distractions and hindrances the world assailed him with. Food was obviously the biggest. Were those chips still in the cupboard? But almost anything could be a distraction if he let it, as he often did. A small ball of dust or a cloud in the sky could be found as a fascinating occupation for the mind, or anything else, so long as he could abstain from writing.

Now, for the record, he wasn't a particularly lazy young man, but merely unmotivated. At least, so he would have others believe. At any rate, the tale slowly continued to grow, even with the amusement of such interesting items as a crumpled receipt, a human tooth, and several large chips of wood. These and other pleasures would occupy his mind, drowning out the nagging pressure of the teacher, whose insatiable appetite for more and more creative work always hung over his head like a precariously placed object. His mother was no great delight either, with her threats of missing hockey practice, the possibility of being grounded, beatings, and the like. And worst of all, the deadline. Nothing could possibly be more paralyzing than putting a time limit on a creative work. He later learned that by repeatedly thumping his head on the desk, he could eliminate all Consciousness, Worries, and, to his great delight, Noises. The latter were his worst enemy when it came to diversions. He drove these thoughts from his mind. It would do no good to think of that now, especially with a Social assignment coming up, and with the deadline almost here…!

Slowly the page was eaten up by the Sea of Words that came flooding from his pen. He had found that, once started he could keep going, and things would come to him. Eventually he had the page mostly filled. How he finally finished he never knew, but without those last few words, his whole life would have fallen apart, he would have been disowned, evicted, fired, and dumped all in the same day. But he had done it. He had finally conquered the Battle with his Mind, and come out wiser from the experience.

Paul liked and frequently used archaisms like "methinks," "whilst," or "betwixt." Even in school assignments he used terms like "as it were" and "I daresay." A Grade 11 Social Studies assignment on nationalism and loyalties contained a paragraph of touching poignancy. Because of its expression of brotherly love as well as its hint of understanding about allegiance to God, we used it as part of the funeral display.

In my life, family has always been a strong influence. I have five brothers and a sister, almost all of whom are older than I am, so I never lacked for advice or input. I've always looked up to my older brothers, and emulated them in some ways. I have only one younger brother, who has Down syndrome. Because of the closeness of our ages, I will likely be the one who will have the duty of taking care of him when my parents are gone. He's always been well-received by friends and neighbours, but if someone were ridiculing him, or hurting him in any way, I'd have to come to his rescue, as it were. …

> *Religion can be [the] most contentious loyalty anyone can have. People are imprisoned, tortured, even murdered because of their faith. When a person's first loyalty is their religion, and the government is in opposition, they are often imprisoned for their beliefs. These occurrences are very real, and are happening all over the world. The reason these people are imprisoned is because God is their first loyalty and when he is your main priority, all other loyalties follow.*

My husband's heart broke going through Paul's things. What spilled out of that overstuffed keepsake box was an intense, imaginative boy, creative and talented. But we'd both become so accustomed to seeing Paul concentrating on these pursuits over the years that we'd taken it for granted. Mike especially, felt he had forgotten too much the eager little boy in the frustration with the unmotivated, unresponsive young man.

Excerpts of a journal Paul kept in his thirteenth year brought bittersweet smiles to the faces of his siblings. But I was disappointed to find no whispers of conscience, no hopes expressed in prayer, no indication that he took seriously God's claim on his life.

I've shown glimpses of Paul's mind and character here that I only discovered going through his Memory Box years after his death. At the time I brought it out, prior to his funeral, I found the contents too confusing to look at for long. How was I to make sense of my son's life when the sweet innocence was slashed apart by the more recent violent words and images? Drawings I found among the things in his room, like the "crust punk" mohawk-styled skulls brought me great anguish. Lyrics to a song he'd written still scorched my memory:

I wanna burn it down!
Everything I've ever known!
The Christmas tree in the center of town,
Ignorance and conformity!
This s---hole town and everything!
I wanna burn it down!
All the things you thought were true!
I wanna burn it down!
All the s--- I take from you!
I wanna burn it down!
Your useless rules and f----- up minds!
I'll tear down your sacred cow!
Everything that you believe!
One day I will tear it down!

Where had we failed, I wailed inwardly, that a boy with such amazing gifts should put them to such malicious use? Which was the real Paul – creative, cheerful, life-loving boy or angry, rebellious punk?

Chapter 12 – A Matter of Law

Besides funeral planning, there were mundane things to attend to — requesting and depositing Paul's final paycheque, applying for life insurance benefits. My husband took care of these but it was my job to cancel Paul's orthodontic appointment scheduled for October 15, the day we would be burying him. Even the subject of his braces was bumpy with a roller coaster of emotions. Early that year, after a nine-month wait for a consultation, we had finally seen the orthodontist. Yes, Paul needed braces and yes, he agreed to pay half of what our dental plan didn't cover. But when he learned eligibility for the plan required he still reside at home, he changed his mind. Eventually, he gave in and braces were installed in June. This was why I'd been angry when he left home in August, without letting us know he was doing so. He was putting us in the awkward position of having to hide his absence from home. I'd tried to tell myself he'd come back when his seasonal job was over, but I doubted he would. Now it was my duty to phone the orthodontist to cancel his third appointment. I waited on hold for long minutes while the stunned receptionist found someone to help me. Clearly, in a practice devoted primarily to children and youth, dealing with a deceased patient wasn't in a normal day's work. They graciously refunded all fees except for the actual braces themselves. Kind gestures like these helped ease our sad duties.

Perhaps the most difficult of my husband's tasks was fielding calls from the police. They were frequently in contact with us, giving updates on progress in the case. The first call came from the officer who'd attended the scene of the accident. He emphasized that police were pursuing the case and that debris from the scene would lead them to the offending vehicle. He assured us the perpetrator would be found and would undoubtedly serve time. Soon they let us know that the car had been found, that a young man had turned himself in, and that he had been arrested. We knew his name and his age — just six years older than Paul. We were told he was released on a modest bail since without a related previous criminal record, he was deemed a low risk for bolting. I had an uncomfortable feeling, knowing the individual was free to move about in the small city of Red Deer. What if we unknowingly encountered him? He was charged with public mischief and failure to give assistance.

Seriously? Mischief? That conjured images of a snickering kid pulling a Hallowe'en prank! My husband thought public mischief seemed to be merely a charge for creating an inconvenience to the police in having to track down the perpetrator. Many of Paul's friends, too, were incensed that more serious charges were not laid in the case of the death of a human being. Had we taken the time to check online, we would have learned differently. But we were in no frame of mind to be researching. Only much later did we learn the charge was a serious one, carrying a maximum penalty of five years in jail. The federal law states:

> *Every one commits public mischief who, with intent to mislead, causes a peace officer to enter on or continue an investigation by*
>
> **(a)** *making a false statement that accuses some other person of having committed an offence;*
>
> **(b)** *doing anything intended to cause some other person to be suspected of having committed an offence that the other person has not committed, or to divert suspicion from himself;*

And the failure to give assistance charge was more serious still.

> *Every person commits an offence who has the care, charge or control of a vehicle, vessel or aircraft that is involved in an accident with*
>
> **(a)** *another person, …*
>
> *and with intent to escape civil or criminal liability fails to stop the vehicle, … give his or her name and address and, where any person has been injured or appears to require assistance, offer assistance. Every person who commits an offence under subsection (1) is guilty of an indictable offence and liable to imprisonment for life if*
>
> **(a)** *the person knows that another person involved in the accident is dead*
>
> *Every person who commits an offence under subsection (1) knowing that bodily harm has been caused to another person involved in the accident is guilty of an indictable offence and liable to imprisonment for a term not exceeding ten years.*

At one point, we were informed the prosecution had added the charge of criminal negligence causing death, carrying a prison sentence of three years to life. This charge seemed to better fit the reality we were facing. But, as one of our sons said, "It won't bring Paul back." And my earlier fears that one of my sons had been the perpetrator of a crime were still so recent I was loathe to see a young man's life shattered with a long prison term. The criminal negligence charge was soon withdrawn, however, due to lack of evidence. The offender would not actually be charged with causing Paul's death. His having fled the scene made criminal negligence or even impaired driving impossible to prove. It was only his behaviour subsequent to the collision for which he'd be held accountable.

Four months later, the preliminary hearing was postponed until October 2013. We were disturbed by a passing comment made by the police constable in charge of the investigation suggesting the prosecution might "make a deal" with the defense if the accused were to enter a guilty plea before trial. This seemed to imply a further reduction in the severity of the charges and resulting penalties. In response to our concerns, the constable wrote, "As a mother, I shed many tears for your son. I was able to come home and hug my sons and my heart ached knowing that you wouldn't be able to, and how unfair that is." She said she never crossed the Taylor Drive bridge without thinking of our son. A better term than "deal," she went on to explain, would have been "resolution." The prosecution hoped for an early guilty plea, not to save court time or bring lenience to the accused but rather to see him "pull out one little shred of decency and admit to his wrong doing." It would also spare us the details and pictures of the collision, "all the while seeing him sitting there maintaining his innocence."

In those early days of rumours flying, the woman who first found Paul that night got in touch through Facebook with our sons, Jonny and Tommy. It must have been an indication of how deeply she'd been moved by the horror of what she witnessed that she made the effort to come to their home to talk to them about it. Jonny told us most of what she said had to do with her distress at the length of time it took emergency help to arrive. Though we later discovered it was only six minutes from her call to their arrival at the scene, time stretches in critical life or death moments. No doubt it seemed an eternity. But I pondered one thing they repeated from the conversation.

"I don't know if you're religious," she said, "but my kids go to a Christian school. He just looked like an angel. He looked so peaceful."

This stranger knew nothing about us. If she'd come to our home, where Bibles are in evidence, I might have suspected her comments were made in an attempt to offer the kind of comfort she might think religious folks would expect. But there was nothing in our sons' appearance or home that would have indicated such a background. What she said seemed to come of a genuine sense of the spiritual. She had seen something. Something about her experience had made a profound impression of the supernatural. But what?

Chapter 13 – Visions and Dreams

It had been a week since that early morning visit by the RCMP. By now the tendrils of tragedy had drawn together our scattered children from Louisiana, Florida and Texas. I had a houseful to feed. This was no problem at all since all week, our beloved church family and neighbours had been bringing meals – a whole turkey, deboned, sliced and deliciously seasoned; a large, complete, tender roast beef dinner; pies; buns; pots of chili; cookies; fruit baskets; cheese and cracker trays. I thought sadly of the family of the driver at fault in Paul's death. No doubt his parents were enduring a shame not readily shared with others, I thought. It was unlikely casseroles of comfort would be arriving in that home.

Our family was gathered in the living room around the corner when I entered the kitchen to begin lunch preparations. What I saw there struck me dumb. To the left of the kitchen sink, superimposed against the yellow wall where no one of flesh-and-blood could have stood, I saw the image of Paul!

He wore a ball-cap sideways and a white T-shirt. And he was smiling wide.

"Hey Mom," he said, in the kind of jaunty voice I hadn't heard from him in a very long time. "You'll never guess who's here!"

That was all.

"I had never in any mood imagined the dead as being so – well, so business-like. Yet there was an extreme and cheerful intimacy," C.S. Lewis wrote, describing a similar experience after the death of his beloved wife Joy. Cheerful intimacy was exactly what impressed me.

What could "here" mean, but heaven, I wondered. Yet I was far from any confident assurance that Paul was with the Lord. But intuitively, I did understand the meaning of this message about who might be with Paul.

A year before Paul's death, I'd had a strong sense that I was to go see an acquaintance in the hospital as he was dying. It seemed urgent that I speak to him about Jesus. In the past, there had been situations where I'd experienced similar promptings which I'd ignored. I came to regret my justifications and rationalizations. Instead, this time I went promptly, repressing my inner objections. Paul, his younger brother Timothy and I piled into the SUV on a gray December day and made the hour-long trip to the hospital. Our friend had been tethered in a wheelchair to the nurses' station to curb his wandering tendencies. He was suffering from oxygen deprivation due to heart failure so he was in and out of lucidity. It had been a disjointed discussion that day and I left only with the assurance that I had obeyed God's prompting. All I could do was pray that God would use the scripture I'd read to him to change his heart.

So now this image. For a long time afterward, I found it puzzling. I knew it wasn't a dream – I had not been sleeping. I had never before seen such a thing. Was it a vision? Considering my anxiety about Paul's eternal state at that time, I knew the joy emanating from my son's face wasn't something I could conjure up. At the same time, I was only too aware that the mind is a mysterious thing and that trauma and emotion can evoke all kinds of states and impressions. As much as I wanted to believe this was God's message to me that Paul was safely with him, I knew powers of association were a factor. Certainly, our late friend's widow had been to our door a few days earlier to bring us a card and a plant.

In the past, people had shared with me stories of supernatural events, coincidences, visions, dreams, or even direct instructions from God. Those who'd experienced these things were sincerely convinced of their genuineness and their heavenly source. God "told" one friend her expected baby would be a girl. Another friend "heard" God bargain with her. She was to lose weight and he would grant her a certain guy as her boyfriend. Less than five years and three children later, they were divorced. Did God answer her prayer because she kept her side of the deal? Or considering how things turned out in the long run, did he fail her by granting her desire?

And why would God reveal this information ahead of time to one Christian and not to another in the same situation? Was it meant to prove that God still speaks directly to us today? I only needed to open my Bible to prove the same thing. Did it prove a closer connection to God in the life of the favoured one?

"Seeing" this image of Paul raised a dilemma for me. Would I rely on a personal experience that gave me desperately needed hope? Or would I trust scripture alone even if it left my questions unanswered? "If private revelations agree with Scripture, they are needless, and if they disagree, they are false," according to Puritan pastor John Owen.

I knew that at the least, thinking we have new revelation from God is simply foolish or mistaken. At worst, however, there can be serious consequences. When a friend's husband was diagnosed with cancer, a church member told them the Lord had assured her "this sickness is not unto death." Weeks later he died and his widow was left trying to figure out why God would have revealed such a thing. Had he only been teasing them? Was he perhaps mistaken? My heart ached for her turmoil at a time when she most needed assurance of God's perfect governing of all life and death matters. Small wonder that in the Bible, false prophets receive strict censure from God.

My personal experience was unverifiable. But it was tempting to attach great significance to it. For some folks, questioning their experience or its source is to doubt the truth of God. I had learned to approach such experiences with caution even though their origin seemed only to be explained supernaturally. God's revelation to mankind in the Bible is complete, lacking nothing. It's not exhaustive – there's still much I don't understand and many questions that aren't answered in it. But it gives us everything we need to know in answer to the critical questions of life – Who am I? Who is God? Where did I come from? Where am I going? What is the purpose of life?

And yet, living in a personal relationship with almighty God is a lifelong supernatural experience. God had often given me nudges and prompts to go a certain direction or avoid a certain action. Most often this gentle guidance had taken the form of a scripture verse popping into the mind. But there had also been dazzling serendipity, a calm assurance of the rightness of a course of action despite risk, a warning against doing the wrong thing or a confident trust that I'd said the right thing.

So, what was I to make of this Paul-sighting? I knew personal experiences had to be defined, controlled and judged by the Bible. If they didn't line up with a sound understanding of the clear teaching of scripture, the fault was with me and my interpretive skills. In his letter to believers, the Apostle Peter speaks of his experience of being on the mountain with Jesus. He and two others were dazzled by the brilliance of Christ's glory. They heard God's booming voice approving his Son. It must have been the most jaw-dropping experience of Peter's life to that point – a momentous new revelation. But when he mentions it in his letter some years later, straightaway he moves to the Word of God as better and more authoritative than his experience. (II Peter 1:16 -21)

The brief experience I had that morning before my son's funeral was something I pondered even though it perplexed me. The illusion of Paul had looked happier and more relaxed than I'd ever seen him. While it gave me hope, it also raised many of the questions I've just described. I relate it now only because I have the chance to describe the context of my emotions at the time and explain the way the Bible governs all such experiences. I kept it largely to myself for two reasons: First, the unreliability of emotional experiences. And second, I feared giving false assurance to others about their own destiny. I didn't want to lead them to think, contrary to scripture, that somehow everyone ultimately gets to heaven or that it doesn't matter whether you reject Christ.

Chapter 14 – Not a Tame Lion

New Year's Day, 2012. I awakened with a sense of dread, thinking this could be the year someone dear to me would die. Naturally my first thought was of my dad who had been degenerating due to Parkinson's disease for almost twenty years.

Snug in our home against the bitter north wind that winter, Mike and I had spent evenings reading a book called *Which None Can Shut* by Reema Goode. The author describes thrilling accounts of Muslims in the closed Islamic countries of the Middle East coming to faith in Christ. At great personal risk, these Muslims were falling like ripe fruit into the lives of Christian missionaries in astoundingly unlikely ways, with seemingly little or no effort on the part of Christians. In the final chapter, the author explains the origin of these widespread conversions. She tells of the lonely labour of missionaries of the past two centuries who served the Muslim people faithfully, sharing with them the good news of Jesus. Despite years of devotion and much hardship they saw only a handful of converts, if any, during their lifetime. Then she describes a wave of concerted world-wide prayer for the Muslim world that took place during the 1980s. I recalled a guest speaker in our church in about 1984 challenging us to pray for Muslims. For a short time, I did so. Goode attributes the current wave of conversions to God's answer to those prayers.

Reading the book, I considered God's behind-the-scenes working in history; how he prompted people to pray for revivals down through the centuries. How he answered those prayers with a great turning of people's hearts toward him at various points in history. And how even today he is accomplishing his purposes in his perfect timing. But what about that critical delay between the concert of prayer and the current movement of faith? I thought with grief of the generations of Muslim people who died without Jesus. Were those lost ones merely disposable? Did they live only so they could have offspring who would be the ones to hear the good news and come to repentance? Were they "sacrificed" as I sometimes "sacrificed" one pair of jeans by using the fabric to mend another pair? It was inevitable then to think of the sons I was praying for. Would God allow one of my sons to fall through the cracks in order to save two others? At that time, my thoughts centred on the possibility of some set-back, perhaps an accident resulting in a temporary disability, that would have a sobering effect on them all. Never once did the death of one of them cross my mind. My journal entry for January 17, 2012 expresses some of my fears:

> *God, in his great sovereignty, moves in ways mysterious to us and answers prayers in his own time. My belief in that, and the awareness that he is the God of eternity, causes me to worry, because he might not save my boys. There were many who died in their sins without Christ while those missionaries worked and prayed and waited. And they never got to see the outpouring,*

> *amazing answer to their prayers. It's that long-range plan that troubles me. What about these individuals that I love and am so concerned about? As much as I rejoice in the prospect of God's perfect timing and sovereign plan to save those of his choice, I fear that some may get lost in the shuffle.*

How intricate are the contingencies and dependencies of every event in life! It frightened me to think of the sweeping, and possibly alarming maneuvers God's answer to my prayers for my family might require. I echoed C.S. Lewis's words, "We are not necessarily doubting that God will do the best for us, we are wondering how painful the best will turn out to be."

I was driven to the same response the Psalmist had on considering God's perfect knowledge and providential plan – "such knowledge is too much for me. It is high; I cannot attain it." (Psalm 139) But in big and little ways I was frequently reminded that God is not only the Almighty Lion of Judah, He is also All-Good. As the children in Narnia said of Aslan,

> *Ooh!" said Susan, "I'd thought he was a man. Is he — quite safe?*
>
> *"Safe?" said Mr. Beaver; "don't you hear what Mrs. Beaver tells you? Who said anything about safe? 'Course he isn't safe. But he's good. He's the King, I tell you."*

I ended that January journal entry with words from my beloved Psalm 73:25, 26:

> *"Whom have I in heaven but You?*
> *And there is none upon earth that I desire besides You.*
> *My flesh and My heart fail;*

But GOD is the strength of my heart and my portion forever."

In February 2012, my mom and I had a rare opportunity to spend time together on a long drive. One of the ways we passed the time was to memorize a section from the Heidelberg catechism of 1563.

Question 27: What do you understand by the Providence of God?
Answer:
Providence is
The almighty and ever present power of God
By which He upholds, as with His hand,
Heaven and earth and all creatures,
And so rules them, that
Leaf and blade
Rain and drought,
Fruitful and lean years,
Food and drink,
Health and sickness,
Prosperity and poverty –
All things in fact, come to us
Not by chance
But from His fatherly hand.

Over and over we repeated those lyrical lines of comfort and assurance, each of us letting the all-encompassing truth of them nurture our souls. For Mom, the future held my dad's inevitable decline with its loss of relationship and heavy load of care-giving, while I carried the concern for sons who I feared were straying from

God. For both my mother and me, these truths provided relief from fear and worry. Allowing them to take root in our minds renewed our confidence in the loving God who held us both in his compassionate hands, no matter what was to come.

Chapter 15 – Totally Depraved?

Was Paul a bad kid? Why did I feel that incongruous, initial relief on receiving the news of the accident? The oppressive weight of vigilance and anxiety over him had lifted. "I'll never have to worry about him again," I told my sister after giving her the news of Paul's death.

Increasingly during his last two years of high school, I had sensed his hostility toward me. It seemed I had to constantly prod him to get off Facebook or quit listening to music and get back to work on his courses. We had the computer in the living room where I could keep an eye on his activities but I hated the role of prison warden. I felt less and less freedom to leave him at home alone, never sure what he might be up to on the Internet.

On one occasion, he eluded me in town and I spent a couple of hours searching for him in stores, the library, at friends' homes – anyplace he might have been. When I finally found him, he offered no apology and his only explanation was he'd gone for coffee with a friend. Another time while he was home alone, he took the liberty of joyriding with only a learner's permit in his brother's unregistered vehicle. Later, he cooked up a plan to buy a family friend's old car. Paul's dad had to veto the transaction by calling the friend directly. It was clear Paul resented the intervention. No matter how much we explained to him the old car was overpriced and would cost him a fortune in fuel and repairs, he saw us as intent on ruining his life. When he wanted to get a job working at a pizza place, I saw it as an opportunity to motivate him. He could do so, I told him, when I saw him faithfully keeping pace with his schoolwork. Nothing changed in the work habit department, so again, I was the wicked witch.

I remember him checking out cell phones in a store. Most kids his age had one. He was far behind on his math that school year so I told him he could have one when he had finished the course. There was no more talk of the phone. So much for my efforts at motivation. I ended up working on math with him right through the summer of Grade 11 for him to be ready for Grade 12.

We did allow one reprieve from summer school that year. We sponsored his mission trip with a youth group headed for ECHO, an experimental farm in Florida dedicated to developing farming methods that will succeed in even the most hostile environments. On the return trip, he had a layover in Indiana where my sister lives. She and her husband were to take him to Chicago airport the next day. As Paul made his way through security, a new spiked wrist band he'd bought in Florida set off the alarm. Since he refused to discard it, he was denied entry. It was fortunate my sister and her husband had not yet left the airport. They took him back home with them and negotiated a second attempt the next day, keeping the offending wristband to mail to him later.

I was furious with Paul. His selfish thoughtlessness had now cost considerable time, effort, money and inconvenience beyond our own family. As a consequence for having messed up, Paul had to write his aunt and uncle a letter of apology. We also required him to delete an obscenely-named Facebook wall he'd been using, which we later learned he didn't do. In addition, he had to dig out an area along one of my flower beds to prepare it for a pathway I hoped to make. Silent and sullen, he met our demands.

Perhaps our biggest concern was a girl. Paul met Samantha at our church and began to hang out with her when he was sixteen. Dark-eyed pretty and well-developed for all to see in her low-cut tops, Sam was only thirteen. Although she attended our church, it seemed she was only there to get away from a difficult home life. More and more often the two of them left the other kids and went off on their own after the church service or youth event.

Knowing some of her background, we had several talks with Paul about her. It seemed futile to talk about purity and preparing to be a wise husband and father. He didn't seem to care much about what the Bible had to say. We focused more on the fact that they were both too young to be pairing off, cutting themselves off from group activities. We told him how troubled her life was, that she needed time to mature and work out some of the difficulties with her parents. The less responsive he became, the more desperate our reasoning. Having a boyfriend, we said, would likely do further damage to her. It could only go two ways – marriage, for which they were both far too young, or end in the pain of a broken relationship. Either way he was diverting her from the important work of growing up and learning to deal with her broken family.

One Halloween night, Paul asked if he could take our SUV to town and go trick-or-treating with his friends. Weary of always saying no to him, we agreed, with a stipulation. He was to stay with the group of kids from youth group and he was not to drive anywhere with passengers, a condition of the graded driver's license he held. I hoped he would have a good time and it could be the beginning of both further trust on our part and further opportunities on his.

About 9:00 p.m. the phone rang. It was his girlfriend's guardian wondering if Paul was home yet and whether Sam was with him. My nerves went on high alert with this news.

"No," I said. "They're not here."

Mike hopped in the car immediately to go to town and search for him.

Are they out somewhere drinking? Have they run off together? I had a runaway of my own – my heart rate! This was just what I'd been afraid of.

A few minutes later, another relative of Sam's called, irate. Seven vehicles of friends and relatives had been out looking all over town for the two, she said.

Great! Just great!

Added to my angst over what Paul and this girl might be up to, I now knew our family would be fine fodder for the small-town gossip mill.

The girl's aunt and uncle had found our vehicle but when they approached it to talk to the pair, Paul had driven off. I explained that my husband had just gone to join the search and I would let her know if and when we found her niece.

My hand shook as I hung up the receiver. I'm probably not unique in my dislike of having people angry at me. And this was serious. I was not acquainted with these people at all, but a nightmare of possibilities terrorized my mind.

Will they get the police involved? What if they charge him with kidnapping? Or statutory rape? Oh Paul!

I had no doubt that the girl was a willing participant in all of this but at fourteen years of age, she was below the age of consent. I went to the computer to research the law on such charges.

Suddenly it occurred to me that Paul might naturally seek refuge with his older brothers. At that time Jonny and Tommy were living in the larger of the two towns nearest us. I rushed to the phone and reached Tommy. I explained the crisis. No, he hadn't seen Paul. I couldn't keep back my frustration at the whole mess and unfairly laid some guilt on him.

"You might want to think about what kind of an example you're setting for him," I snapped before I hung up.

At that moment, the front door opened. In walked Sam and Paul. I stared at him with what I hoped was a burning look. Neither of them said anything. Fearing they might turn right around and leave again if I let my feelings show, I held out my hand for the keys.

"You are in deep trouble. Very deep trouble. Sam's family are all out looking for her, and Dad just left to hunt for you," I told him, keeping my voice low. "I'll take her home and then we'll deal with you."

I grabbed my jacket and Samantha followed me meekly enough out to the SUV.

We drove for a few moments in silence. My own past sins when I was about her age raced through my mind. I remembered the fear and shame I felt at age fifteen as my friend's dad drove us home one night after we had been caught shoplifting. Facing my parents' disappointment and anger had been horrible.

Now I had fifteen minutes with this girl captive in my vehicle and I figured I'd make them count. I started out with a story. I told the courtship story of a young friend of ours who had waited a long time for the right man to come along while peers were out dating at far younger ages. I told of her first kiss on her wedding day, of the purity and beauty of that love and how it would create a foundation for a marriage of trust and intimacy.

As silent as Paul usually was, I was surprised to find this girl quite responsive. She didn't know any of her relatives cared enough about her to go searching for her, she said. She also told me she and Paul had not had sex.

As we approached town and slowed down, I realized I didn't know where she lived. She could have pointed me toward any house and I'd never know if that were really her home. I began to fear she might just hop out at any given stop sign. I'd be left trying to explain both my son's actions as well as her still-missing status.

But she didn't. She directed me to her aunt's home. No vehicles were in the driveway. Maybe I could quietly drop her off and leave without having to face irate family members. Before getting out, I asked if I could pray with her and she agreed. I asked God to give her courage to face her guardians and to help her trust him with her life. Silently, I asked him to give me courage to face her folks as well.

We were walking up to the house when a man came out on the low deck. He loomed large and silent above us, his long curly hair backlit by the porch light. Such a creepy exaggerated silhouette did nothing to bolster my confidence. As I introduced myself, his wife came out too. She seemed glad to see Sam and friendlier than on the phone previously. I made my apologies and left as soon as I could.

On the way home, I agonized over how we should handle this misdemeanor. I half wished Sam's family would call the police. Sometimes a brush with the law can put a scare into a thoughtless teenager. At the very least I hoped Paul had seen the criminal justice web page I'd left open on the computer. We learned later he had called his brother and expressed fear that he might go to jail.

At home, we emphasized to him the serious charges that could result. His only explanation was that Sam had told him she was afraid of her relatives, that they had seemed angry when they caught up with him, so he had tried to help her escape them.

It was only months after his death that the significance of his having brought her home to us dawned on me. He was trying to protect her and he felt our home was a refuge; that perhaps we would have answers or could offer help. It was evidence of his merciful and protective nature. It was also a clear sign of his trust in us. I wish I'd recognized these virtues then so I could have at least commended him on his good intentions.

Paul's punishment, we determined at the time, would be a complete ban on our vehicle for an indefinite time. He would also have to make an apology in person to Sam's family, an event we dreaded at least as much as he likely did. This was a boy whose resistance to apologizing, even as a preschooler, had made an impression on me. I had never been able to understand it. He would be trembling and visibly fighting tears yet remaining close-mouthed, preferring a spanking to saying he was sorry to his brother.

I can still see him, on the afternoon before our scheduled visit to go see Sam's aunt and uncle, sitting, seemingly disconsolate, on the kitchen floor with his back against the kitchen cabinets. I knew something of the turmoil of anxiety and humiliation that must have been raging inside him.

I told him about my own delinquency at age fifteen. And I told him about my parents' insistence that I return the stolen items and apologize in person to the store manager. It had been awkward and humiliating and the manager hadn't made it any easier, adding a lengthy, stern warning of her own. But, I told Paul, doing it had lifted a huge burden off my shoulders. It would do the same for him if he were truly sincere, I said. Though he said nothing in response, I hoped it wasn't just my imagination that his attitude seemed to soften.

That evening we went to their home for Paul to make his apology. Though it was an uncomfortable meeting, Sam's folks were welcoming and understanding and, if anything, made it too easy for him. I wondered if he'd benefit when they simply excused his actions as one of those crazy things kids do sometimes.

Our next interchange with them was a couple of weeks later when I received another phone call from Sam's guardian describing a private Facebook conversation she'd intercepted between Paul and her niece. It contained veiled threats by the girl against her family, stating they were "an accident waiting to happen." In his return message Paul had sympathized with her, although, surprisingly, he hadn't responded in kind with words of resentment against us. Now the guardian wondered if she should notify police. I agreed that she should.

She did report it but the officer simply told her it was a common thing amongst teens. No big deal, she was told. I didn't *want* Paul to have a record or get involved with the police in any way. But I looked at it as a chance to shake him up a bit; to cause him to think about his life and the direction he was headed. It did at least give us the leverage we needed to insist Paul finally change the indecent name on his Facebook account.

One night not many weeks later at just past midnight, I woke to a phone call from police.

"Do you know where your son is?" a female officer wanted to know.

Jolted from sleep in that way, I wasn't sure of anything. I thought he was upstairs sleeping in his room. Yes, his shoes were at the front door, his jacket hung up on the coat tree.

"His girlfriend is missing," the officer said. "Can you ask him if he knows anything about it?"

I went up to Paul's room and woke him. No, he said, about as sleep-befuddled as I had been. Sam had said nothing to him about planning to leave home.

I relayed that to the police. Not long later they called back to say the girl had been found. Paul was particularly sluggish the next day. He explained he hadn't been able to sleep at all that night, worried about Samantha. He had gone back to bed, and I assumed, to sleep after the first call. I should have told him about the second call letting us know all was well.

My fear and worry over their relationship kept me from seeing the truly caring heart Paul had toward that girl. I completely missed his merciful, tenderness toward the unfortunate. Now I wonder what God might have done with that attribute had Paul lived.

* * *

That winter, 2011-12, I continued to drive Paul to hockey or youth events rather than allowing him the use of our vehicle. I hated having to do this, treating him like a child and distrusting him. And I could think of better ways to spend my time. Yet he had never apologized to us for his irresponsible caper nor expressed any intention to be trustworthy. We couldn't know what his thoughts were; we could only go by his actions.

Years after his death, I thought further about Paul's difficulty apologizing, even as a preschooler. It seemed it was the hardest thing ever. Neither gentle persuasion nor punishment could make him do it. Now I put that together with another memory - his dread of speaking in front of people. One night, my husband had brought topic cards for impromptu speeches to the supper table to try injecting some lighthearted learning to an otherwise silent, grim ritual. With a two-minute time limit, Mike and I took our turn with topics like "What fashion trend you followed was very cool then but now looks ridiculous?" or "Which language would you like to speak fluently?" Then it was Paul's turn.

He took a card and read the topic. For more than a minute we sat in silence, waiting. When he opened his mouth, I thought he'd start talking, but he closed it again in a tight line. The silence became uneasy.

"Just start talking," we told him. "We're a sympathetic audience. You saw the mistakes we made."

But it was only a moment before he flung the card on the table and stormed away from the table. Knowing you can't force someone to have fun, I was frustrated with him at the time. Now I wonder. *Was it more than mere teenage belligerence that made him give up? Was the spoken word truly a terrifying thing for him?* And how did that fit with the motor-mouth he used to be? Some of our other children have told me they suffer from the same tendency to freeze up. They can relate to Paul's reluctance to speak before people, though they can't explain why. I'm left with the unanswerable question, what could we have done to help him overcome this?

So, was Paul a "bad kid"? Are any of us "bad'? None of us are as bad as we could possibly be. By human standards, Paul wasn't bad at all. But God's measuring rod is different. Like a deadly microscopic bacterium in a dish of purest vanilla ice cream, sin taints every aspect of us, making us incapable of choosing or doing good without wrong motives (Romans 3:10-19). What I failed to see in those years of fear and worry over the direction Paul's life was taking was God's unlimited, overpowering love and mercy for sinners.

Chapter 16 – One Last Look

The small black-based lamp with the taupe shade on the table in the funeral chapel foyer was identical to one I had bought at our town's huge annual rummage sale three weeks before. Could it really be mere weeks since I was immersed in happy plans for our ongoing house renovation — when the biggest problem we faced was how to construct the hand-rail of our new L-shaped stairway? Now the ground under our lives had quaked in a seismic shift. I clung to those former familiar pleasures that represented the blessed ordinary. Yet my grasp was being pried off them. We were here to view the body of our son.

We went downstairs where a heavy tapestry curtain partitioned off the back of a small meeting room set up like a church sanctuary. Several of our sons were there already. As we awaited the arrival of the rest of our family in separate vehicles from the neighbours' home where they were staying, I intruded on a tender moment between my husband and one of our boys.

"I just want you to know I love you," Mike told him as the two passed each other in the hallway leading to the washroom. I had often reminded my husband, perhaps even nagged him, to express his love to our boys. Like the green sprig of a plant growing through a crack in barren rock, for me this was a glimpse of something good coming out of tragedy.

I was most surprised to see my husband's only brother arrive at the funeral home. We had had little contact in the five years since my father-in-law's death in 2007. I was touched that he felt this was an important enough event to make the fourteen-hour trip.

The funeral director met us and explained we could go one by one, or as a group, behind the curtain where Paul lay in his casket. Which did we prefer, she wanted to know. Choices, decisions seemed beyond us. Somehow my husband and I found ourselves alone together with that formidable box in front of us. I noticed the names of far-away friends on flower arrangements clustered around the casket. We approached with unease.

Lying on the white pillowing was … someone. Someone who wore the blue dress shirt I had pressed. Someone wearing the toque we had provided to the funeral home. Someone with a single four-inch lock of neon green hair escaping the front edge of that toque.

But who? Who was this stranger with the obvious heavy make-up on his face? Whose eyebrows were marked by smudges of colour darker than Paul's eyebrows had ever been, leaving his natural, long eyelashes looking pale and gray by contrast. I searched his face, vainly trying to find the boy I knew. The lips were full and almost protruding, where Paul's had been thin. The nose was wide and thick. Paul's had been narrow and fine. One cheekbone was sunken flat, lopsided and out of balance to the other.

I turned to Mike and saw the same confused question in his eyes. *Is this even Paul?*

"But if this isn't him, where is he?" I asked. A spark of hope glimmered inside me. Perhaps there had been a mistake! But common sense made a recovery, extinguishing that hope. The police wouldn't make a mistake like this. Paul had been carrying his wallet with identification. There was no mistake. Part of the confusion, no doubt, was due to the strangeness of death, the unnatural rending of spirit from body. A corpse isn't referred to as "the departed" for no reason. Even funerals I've been to where the person is recognizable are fraught with the inescapable fact that the deceased is no longer there.

At last I saw the scar on the chin. The only stitches Paul ever received had been in that exact spot. When he was about eighteen months old he had become restless in church and I had taken him out to the back of the meeting place. Since it kept him quiet, I was letting him toddle around on the shiny tile floor when he tripped on a sound system cable and split his chin open. He howled and blood gushed. But at Emergency, he only watched in grave silence while the doctor anesthetized and stitched closed the gash.

And now I looked at his hands. I recognized the long-fingered, strong hands of a guitar player. It was Paul, but a strangely altered, barely recognizable Paul.

Would I feel any familiarity if I touched him? For a moment I wondered if that were allowed. But I had carried him in my body! He was my baby and I had nursed him for fifteen months! I pressed my hands to his chest. There was no warmth or give and I felt the crinkle of paper. Paper? I later realized there was a huge Y-shaped autopsy wound, necessary to determine exact cause of death. It would have had to be covered with some sort of bandage.

It seemed neglectful somehow to turn our backs on him and I felt blameworthy for my lack of tears. But how could I cry for this unfamiliar stranger? No further purpose was served by our presence there – no matter how my heart called out to him, he was not going to respond. Besides, others were waiting their turn for a moment alone with him.

By ones and twos, they somberly passed behind the curtain, his brothers and sister in their turn, then the rest of our family members.

"What a last memory to have of Paul," Tommy said. "I'll never get that out of my head."

Our next dilemma was whether Timothy should go in.

"He certainly doesn't need that," was one person's opinion.

We asked the funeral director her advice. She hesitated to instruct us, only suggesting that some people found including children in every aspect of the grieving process was helpful while others chose not to. Again, we were faced with a seemingly insurmountable decision for which we were inexperienced and unprepared.

We turned to our pastor. He too was reluctant to direct us. But finally, he said we knew our son best, and suggested it might be helpful if we went in with Timothy and explained things to him. We had to prod Timo a little, and he seemed apprehensive about getting very close to the coffin. My memory of what Mike explained to him is vague now, but I recall Timo's sober silence and stoic demeanor. When we asked if he had questions, characteristically he said nothing. I wished we could know what was going through his mind.

Rejoining the rest of our family gathered in this rare way, I longed to spend more time together. Perhaps we could go out for coffee afterward. But then I tried to imagine how, after what we'd just seen, we would be able to talk and kibbutz and carry on as we liked to do. We went home that evening without my even suggesting going out, loss upon loss.

Chapter 17 – A Father's Regrets

How do you choose what to wear to your son's funeral? Mostly, I just didn't want to go. Yet both my husband and I were all too aware that this was the one and only chance we would have to publicly pay tribute to Paul. There would be no wedding or other landmark occasion where we could honour him.

When we pulled up to the front of the church beside the funeral home limousine, into parking spots reserved for family, flashes of glitter and colour caught my eye. There, on the left side of the church entrance, was the punk contingent, turned out in full regalia. It felt like an assault, their arriving in costumes that screamed the very rebellion I felt had put Paul in harm's way. At least, that was my initial gut reaction. Their appearance, intentionally shocking and offensive, was so tightly entwined with the cause of our loss, I was aghast that they seemed unaware of the connection. But as the service went on, the Spirit of God whispered through my offended mood with compassion only he could give. He urged me to see them through God's eyes: lost and confused kids, hurting at the loss of a friend. Of the more than two hundred gathered to remember Paul, they were the emptiest of answers to the sufferings of life, the least equipped to understand death or to deal with grief.

It's a measure of my bewilderment that I was overjoyed to see family and friends I hadn't seen in years yet disappointed that we would not get the chance to visit. I caught sight of a line-up of young guys in hockey jerseys – Paul's team with their two coaches. Only now do I recognize how tumultuous, how conflicted were the emotions this evoked. Where I should have been honoured they were identifying with him and taking the time to remember him fondly, all I could think was how very alive they all looked and how final it all was for Paul. He would never glide onto the ice with them again.

When we walked into our familiar church auditorium, I looked up to see a large picture of Paul projected onto the wall at the front and the brutal reason we were there pierced through me. Below the pulpit was his flower-covered casket. What irony that he was now at the center of attention in a place he'd so recently told us he didn't want to be. Just six months earlier, he had stubbornly remained seated in a church service while everyone else stood to sing. Now all these people overflowing our church's sanctuary and filling the fellowship hall had taken time off work to be with us, to honour Paul, to remember. What I wanted more than anything was to escape.

"We are gathered here today to bid farewell to Paul Bertin – to honour his memory and to celebrate his life - which within the parameters of normal human rationale was far too short," Pastor Ross began.

There was music – harp and the singing of Paul's favourite hymns. We sang O Worship the King, a piece Paul had played on his cello with Jonny on violin, but it was the second hymn, Leaning on the Everlasting Arms, that choked me. Mike had often sung it to Paul at bedtime when he was a baby.

Together, the congregation read aloud the words of one hymn that perfectly expressed what was carrying me through that day.

> *With mercy and with judgment my web of time He wove;*
> *And aye the dews of sorrow were lustered with His love*
> *I'll bless the hand that guided, I'll bless the heart that planned,*
> *Enthroned where glory dwelleth in Immanuel's land.*

Some of those present might have found it hard to imagine Paul had hymn favourites. *Had we presumed too much? Like the caption on the funeral bulletin,* Safe in the Arms of Jesus, *were we giving a false impression of who Paul was?*

Eulogy literally means "good word." Could anyone guess how conflicted I was at having to say a good word about a son of whom I felt shame? All too soon, it was time for Mike and me to give ours. My legs seemed unwilling to budge when we were first called on. *I don't know how to do this, Lord, help me!*

Mike was the first to speak.

> *We're here today to remember Paul and to pay tribute to him. Some of you have known Paul all his life. Some of you have never met him. We appreciate the fact that you're here. But what we'd like to do today, while we can't cram eighteen years into merely a few minutes, is to share some of the highlights of Paul's life and some of our own thoughts and memories about him.*
>
> *I hope you'll forgive us if we go a little long and have some trouble getting through this.*

When Paul was born, he hit the ground running. It's a remarkable thing, this child, moments after birth, lying on his mother's stomach and raising his head.

The following morning, I was doing what new fathers do, carrying him around and what you do with a newborn baby is, you support their head. So that's what I was doing, having had five before Paul. I was amazed that he raised his head from my shoulder. He began looking around. I was immediately struck by the fact that he was strong, he was alert and he was curious. He was yet unnamed. It struck me at that point, "This is Paul."

I had been going through some things at that time in my own life about theology, about philosophy. And I had been greatly impressed by Paul, the apostle, and what the Bible records about his life, the kind of man he was. Strong, tenacious, passionate. I just had a sense that I was holding another Paul in my hands and we named him Paul as a result.

As he grew, we began to see his character emerge. A few adjectives that I've chosen that are accurate to describe the characteristics we saw in Paul's life:

He was intense. Those of you who know him, know what I mean.

He was passionate.

He was curious.

He was adventurous.

He was creative.

He was detailed and talented.

Early, he showed his love for music. His mother will tell you that he didn't sleep well. And so, it required we sing him to sleep at times. That is a pleasant memory I have of singing Paul to sleep.

He really liked "Silent Night." When it came to the line "sleep in heavenly peace," he came to respond, "green peas." In time, he would anticipate that line before I even got to it. Still further, he would request the song, "Green Peas."

What he did, he did passionately. One of the early memories I have is of him at our square coffee table with a great big container of little cars. He would pull these cars out in great number, twenty or thirty, and drive each car to the corner of the table. Then he'd proceed to back up one car and drive it to the next corner, getting down at eye level to watch as each one went. I have no idea what was going on in his mind but it was something active. This was not a mindless thing.

A little later, he began to draw things and catalogue them. It was amazing to us and still is.

He was fascinated with The Lord of the Rings and with The Chronicles of Narnia and he created his own worlds. The countries even had hockey teams with names and logos which he drew.

He had never been all that interested in athletics but suddenly, because his older brothers were interested in hockey, he caught the bug. The Calgary Flames were going for the Cup and he suddenly became passionate about that. And I mean passionate! This was vitally important to him. I'll tell you, the tears were bitter in game seven when the Flames lost!

But that was Paul. If he did it, he did it passionately. He did it intently. There was nothing half-way about him.

His play included acting these things out. Not everything he did was intellectual. He actually got out a sword and acted these things out.

We noticed a cute thing one day: We have this little spruce tree in our yard that we planted when a neighbour let us transplant some from her yard. The prettiest one, we put in a prominent place in our yard with great hopes this was going to be a lovely tree.

Well, here was my creative, active son, sword in hand, fighting this mighty foe, which was the tree. That was Paul for you. I didn't spend a lot of time thinking about it. It was cute.

Until later.

I came back and found he had defeated this foe!

The audience laughed.

I didn't find it cute at that point. For me, it was not a pleasant memory anymore. It was a disappointment. I was mad at him. I said something like, "How could you do something so irresponsible?" I was distressed over what I saw as permanent, irreparable damage to this beautiful little tree!

Over time, we got used to the tree that way. It is what it is.

Now, I want to leave you with hope.

We didn't have hope for that tree. We just accepted it. But in this tree is a lesson. One that is meaningful to me at this point and that I hope will be meaningful to the rest of you.

Who is it that makes the tree grow? Isaiah 61 tells us that God will heal the brokenhearted and comfort those who mourn. And that he will give beauty for ashes. My little tree was ashes.

That little tree today is more beautiful than before Paul vanquished it. You see, God is in the restoration business. And as I say this I want to be abundantly clear. I'm not suggesting in any way that we'll ever see Paul again in this life. That's not what I mean by restoration.

But what I mean is that those of us who remain and who hurt – and we do – will be restored. Because that's the business that God is in.

We sometimes react to the rules. We think that's all religion is about. That's all God is about is rules.

But that's not what it is. It's about restoration and that's really the point.

Chapter 18 – A Good Word?

My husband's transparency in sharing his feelings and failures emboldened me. I knew what it cost him to admit his impatience with Paul and the overwhelming regret that went with it. But as we watch the funeral video years later, we both marvel that we had the calm presence of mind to speak. Truly, the grace of God supported us.

It was my turn next.

> *"Paul was born at home in Okotoks just after midnight, May 7, 1994,"*

I began. Looking out at the crowded church just then, I caught sight of my mother, triggering a memory that I spontaneously added.

> *"My mother was with us for Paul's birth and she's here now. It was a more difficult birth than the others and I remember saying to Mom, 'It hurts.' And it still hurts now."*

I described Paul's remarkable strength as a baby, and the reason we gave him his name.

We could have guessed that from that wiry beginning," I continued, "he would be crawling at five and a half months. With five older children to look after, I was in no hurry for him to get mobile, but apparently, he was. And so his toddlerhood went, just trying to keep an active little boy from harm. Someone asked us not long after he was born, didn't the baby stage get kind of old, since he was the sixth. We told him that if anything, our joy was increased because there were so many to share it with. His brothers and sister found him endlessly entertaining, and of course, a welcome distraction from homeschooling.

By eighteen months, Paul had learned the alphabet and each letter's sounds. I was surprised one day when Paul was three, by something that happened while I was helping Jonny sound out a word.

'Huh –uh- tuh,' Jonny said. 'What's a huh-uh-tuh?'

My husband held up a large card with the letters **hut** printed on it.

From over the arm of the chair, Paul popped up and said in confidential tones, 'It's a pizza store.'

The congregation's laughter sounded to me like the release of pent-up emotion.

Timothy, our youngest, was born when Paul was three. The ladies of the church had planned a baby shower for me and as I was getting ready to go, Paul came down the stairs carrying a towel and wearing his swim trunks.

'I want to go to the shower too,' he said.

More laughter.

Once when Paul was sick and lying on the couch, Danny walked by and said, 'It's kind of nice to see Paul sick – the rest of the time he's just a blur.'

As soon as Paul could read, new worlds opened to him. He loved Garfield comics and pretty much had them memorized. Having learned to read strictly phonetically, there were some surprising comments at times.

'I've gained weight,' Paul announced at the dinner table one day. 'Don't expect me to be wearing –

Here Mike held up another card, this time imprinted with the word **bikini**

– bickinny briefs at the beach anytime soon.'"

This was a boy who pursued his interests intensely and thoroughly. For a while, he was interested in jewels and gems. He studied the encyclopedia and knew every gemstone as well as the names of all the jewel cuts. He drew the Jewish High Priest's jeweled ephod with all the gems labeled and enjoyed looking in the windows at jewelry stores, which I didn't mind either.

He made pages of alphabetized lists of every kind of animal he found in the encyclopedia. Then there was a phase where Paul was fascinated by all things medieval. He filled pages and pages with catalogued listings of real and imaginary weaponry, all neatly labeled, and he was usually seen wearing a shiny silver cape and wielding a homemade wooden sword.

On family vacations, Dad used to buy a large package of red licorice and periodically toss some to the back of the van to appease the natives. Then when we'd stop at restaurants I guess we weren't paying close enough attention because when Paul could help himself to any drink he wanted, he always chose Pepsi. That combination of sugar and red dye …let's just say, 'Energizer Bunny on Steroids.'

When Paul was eight or nine, he went through a phase of gathering clues and making top-secret plans. He filled notepad after notepad with numbers. Serial numbers, model numbers, product codes, wattage and amperage numbers … You'd be sitting at a desk and there he'd be, craning his head under the seat to write down the chair's serial number. There were drawings of elaborate three-story forts. I don't know if we realized what it was all about at the time, but a few years later, I came across one of those notebooks and glanced through it. On the front page, in Paul's neat printing, the heading read: 'Plans for World Domination.'

Once we moved to the country in 2003, there was the fun of having pets. Everyone loved the cats and their numerous kittens but Paul kicked it up a notch by charting an exhaustive genealogy of all the cats we've owned, their inter-breeding and their tragic deaths or disappearances.

Of course, there were always chores to do and Paul, with his preoccupied mind, had to be reminded often. In the days before we had a ride-on mower, when he was about twelve, I asked him to get on with mowing the lawn.

'Come on, Paul,' I said, 'are you a man or a mouse?'

He muttered in reply, 'I'd rather spread disease than mow the lawn.'

Always musical, as a baby, Paul used to love it when Dad sang to him at bedtime. He drove us all crazy as a preschooler, listening to certain tapes over and over until we put a set of headphones on him. That reduced it to the first phrase of each line of a song as he sang along, but couldn't quite keep up. As he got older, I particularly enjoyed singing hymns with him in the van because he could carry the tune while I sang harmony.

When he was six, Paul started cello lessons which he kept up for three years. At one point, we considered having him join an orchestra. He arrived there, settled himself in the cello section and surprised us by playing right along with them all, a piece he'd never seen or heard. He admitted to me not long ago that he hadn't even been touching the strings with the bow but had just faked it the whole time. Still, music was important to him and he took piano and guitar lessons more recently. He picked up the guitar quickly and naturally.

Since 2009, when Paul told us he was interested in becoming an architect, he was working on completing high school. I always enjoyed the way he could turn a phrase. His English essays and creative writing were particularly entertaining.

In the summers of 2010 and 2011, Paul went to Florida to volunteer for a few weeks at ECHO, an experimental farm that works to find ways to help families around the world raise food under difficult growing conditions. It was the first time he'd flown alone and the connections were rather unusual. He missed a flight and found himself in Atlanta airport. From there he called his aunt and uncle in Indiana. They referred him to his cousin Esther who lived in Atlanta and she put him up for the night and got him a flight the next morning. We were amazed that none of this seemed to faze him. He enjoyed getting to know the other young volunteers and the work at ECHO, even the nasty jobs. He told with great enthusiasm about the time he and his buddy had to clean out the sludge from the bottom of the duck pond. Apparently, it deteriorated into a muck-flinging competition and … that's all we'll say about that.

This past summer, Paul was disappointed that diploma exams kept him from going back to ECHO, but he spent Monday evenings volunteering with Special Olympics softball. He was good at motivating Timo to practice batting and catching, and he enjoyed the quirkiness of the disabled athletes.

During his high school years, he and I spent a lot of time together, not all of it in harmony. Sometimes I'd give him a hug, whether I felt like it or not, and he would stiffen or turn away. But after he left home, the week before he died, something had changed. We'd had a birthday celebration for his dad and when we were saying goodbye and I hugged him, he hugged me back.

That was the last time I saw him. It is so encouraging to have a loving final memory."

It was while preparing my eulogy when that last, pleasant memory of Paul came to mind. It seemed so little to go by, so subjective and uncertain. In fact, I wouldn't have even given hugs that night, I was that perturbed with Paul for not living at home as he should have been. But I followed my mother-in-law's good example and hugged all three of my boys before we parted. Paul's return squeeze was unusual enough to make an impact. I'd become accustomed to being met with all the passion of a fencepost when I hugged him. His embrace that day was so significant I recounted the incident to my mom a few days afterward. I was puzzled at the difference from his usual response, yet pleased. *But what did it mean? Did he regret his having left home without our approval?*

To me, the glaring omission from either of our eulogies was the lack of any mention of faith on Paul's part.

Chapter 19 – The Last Goodbye

Before our eyes in the slide show our son Tommy had assembled, my chubby, bright-eyed baby grew into a toddler with a blond bowl-cut, and from there into a busy, sword-wielding, playful boy. I cringed anew at the stark darkness of a few shots of him in punk garb. The final slide showed the tree Paul had vanquished, now full and thriving. Set to the achingly beautiful melody of Come to Jesus, by Chris Rice, the yearning lyrics evoked a tidal wave of emotion in me. The first lines could have been written expressly for Paul — a helpless sinner, abandoned to death. If only the rest of the song were true of him too! It promises sin's weight lifted, its stain blood-washed, and it sings of the sinner freed, laughing in Glory.

When our oldest son, Ben, went to the piano to play Brahms's beautiful Intermezzo in E flat Major, Opus 117 No. 1, he first read its German inscription and gave a translation:

> *Schlaf sanft mein Kind, schlaf sanft und schön!*
> *Mich dauert's sehr, dich weinen sehn.*

(Sleep sweetly my child, sleep gentle and beautiful!
I am very sorry to see you cry.)

Pastor Ross opened his remarks with a bit of background about us. "The Bertin family began attending [our church] about a year ago and Paul came with them. I see a family that is diverse, but close – parents that are intently interested in serving God and developing and maintaining a Christian dynamic within the family. So much so that their approach toward the driver of the vehicle that took Paul's life is one of forgiveness – not vengeance.

"Paul came and went fairly quietly but whenever I talked with him or greeted him I received a respectful and friendly response. Paul graduated this year and in my prayer for the grads I included prayer for all their endeavors from music to education. For like my children – like many of our children – Paul had musical talent and a passion for the same.

"Paul was at that age when he had not yet found out who he really was – that stage of life when muscles are flexed and wings are spread and parents are not quite sure about the flight plan. Sadly no one will really know for sure now because of his tragic and untimely demise. Would he have pursued music in lifelong fashion – would he have returned to his plan to be an architect? Would he have entered mission work as he did for two summers in his earlier teens?

"But I do know this – Paul, in the short time he lived in Red Deer made many friends – a few of whom I have in common – they all regard him as talented, kind and likable."

"Life is a stern teacher," he continued. "It gives the test first and then the lesson. Recognize that grief is a process – not a point in time. And you may not believe it, but though you will never get over this tragedy you can get through it. God has so designed us that painful realities and pleasant memories live at the same address.

Today, painful realities have the run of the house and pleasant memories are forced into a corner while you deal with your pain and hurt and confusion. But eventually, painful realities will be found in the guest room in the basement and pleasant memories will fill the rest of the house…but it will take time."

Pastor Ross went on to remind us of Jesus' promise that he would always be with us.

Following our son's casket out of the church woke feelings in me beyond description. So many faces in the packed-to-capacity church surprised and pleased me, but again, the bleak reason for the presence of so many folks from the past blared through my foggy senses. I turned to face the shoulders of the Paul-bearers – four of our sons, our son-in-law and my brother – who would lift the coffin into the waiting hearse.

There was a short break during which we, the family, were to eat a light lunch prepared by the women of our church. I was touched to see they had decorated the tables with muted beige cloths and wheat in small vases. But I had little appetite for any of the wide variety of food provided. Soon people came into the fellowship hall, offering hugs and condolences. There were so many. I was grateful not much was required of me in response. Some told stories about Paul.

Don, a friend from our former home town, laughingly told the story of a comment six-year-old Paul made about Don's wife.

"Mrs. M. sure must like ketchup chips."

"What makes you say that?" asked our friend.

"Her hair's exactly the same colour," Paul had replied.

How confused and skewed was my outlook on Paul at the time, that I had trouble finding the humour in this. All that came to mind was the insensitivity of the kid's remark and how I'd failed to teach him discretion.

Several from the punk community made a special point to express condolences. One young man gave me a heart-felt hug, saying he, himself, had a young son and couldn't imagine the pain of losing him. I struggled to separate my antipathy toward the cause their costumes promoted, from the love God wanted me to show them as individuals. Some hard feelings must have emerged when I told one young woman that I couldn't like what Paul had been involved in because "punk killed my kid." I remember, too, expressing to another punk girl that Paul must have hated me. She protested strongly, but how did she know he didn't, I wondered.

One of the last people to greet me was a young neighbour who waited in line a long time to tell me, in tears, how he remembered playing floor hockey with Paul in our basement years before.

There was one person that offered me unique encouragement. The mother of a friend of Paul's former girlfriend told me she had been able to have some meaningful talks with the girl in the previous week. During their conversations, Samantha had told her, "We never had sex. Paul said he wouldn't until I was older." It wasn't the commitment to purity I would have wished to hear, but perhaps it was an indication Paul had taken to heart the warnings we gave him about his relationship with her. If he had heard those cautions, could he have been listening to the other things we taught him as well?

After the last sympathizer had come through the line, it was time for the interment. The funeral procession made its slow journey east out of town to the small country cemetery we'd chosen. I'd only been there once before, for the funeral of a neighbour, but I'd found the rural setting surrounded by tall trees intimate and rustic. A smaller crowd came with us: our family, extended family, and almost the entire colourful punk contingent. We crunched through fallen leaves, their dusty-sweetness scenting the still air as we gathered at the gaping hole in the ground. Its edges and the pile of soil surrounding it were sanitized by a drape of green Astroturf. The men carried the coffin to the frame suspended above the grave.

Mike and I each placed a single white rose on the casket.

Pastor Ross gave a few last words, quoting John 11:25. "I am the resurrection and the life. He who believes in Me, though he may die, he shall live. And whoever lives and believes in Me shall never die. Do you believe this?"

"Dear family and friends, death has invaded and taken from this world your beloved son, brother, grandson, nephew, and friend Paul Bertin… His soul lives on, but it has become our duty to commit his physical remains to this grave. Earth to earth, ashes to ashes, dust to dust.

"As we commit Paul's body to this grave we entrust his soul and ourselves to God - our maker, Father, and redeemer; we maintain a sure hope of the return of the Lord Jesus, the resurrection of the body from the grave and a joyful and eternal life in heaven's glory to all who place their trust in him.

"Now unto him that is able to keep you from falling, and to present *you* faultless before the presence of his glory with exceeding joy, To the only wise God our Savior, *be* glory and majesty, dominion and power, both now and ever. Amen." (Jude 24, 25)

And it was over; all the final tasks, loose ends tied up, financial matters and estate attended to, our responsibilities in preparing for the service and burial, and Paul's life on earth.

He lived eighteen years, four months and twenty days. Just 6,727 days; 161,448 hours.

Before we had time to consider or reflect, "Trixie," the funeral director came toward us holding out a bundle of felt markers. Would it be alright if she offered these to anyone who would like to write a parting message on the coffin?

We had only moments to consider the idea. *Write on the beautiful wood of that casket? More defacing graffiti by the predominantly punk crowd? But what difference could it make? It's all going to be covered by dirt and ultimately rot away!* Even thinking about the future end of Paul's coffin was a horrible concept, let alone the thought of what would happen to his body. But there was no real reason to object and I realized it could be an important gesture for the kids who'd attended the graveside service with us. We agreed.

While the young people crowded around, writing their farewells, one of them started playing punk music from an iPhone in his truck parked nearby. This was disturbing. The angry sounds seemed an assault on the solemnity of the setting. I tried to keep from being offended by telling myself this was his best attempt at expressing his grief. Maybe anger at the enemy, Death, wasn't so far out of line if we remember what brought it into this world: Sin. But I wished he wouldn't remind us of the rebellion Paul had been involved in. Much later, some of our children remarked on the disrespect they felt when the punk community "took over" the funeral with their music and desecrated the coffin with their words.

"It's like they were making him their own martyr," one of our children said.

A couple of the young people tore patches off their jackets to leave on the casket in addition to their messages.

"Never will I forget you, 'the kid,'" one wrote. "Keep it up with the greats up there. Oi, brother."

"I love ya, home-schooler. I wish I'd had more time with you. I will forever wave at fires."

As the cemetery emptied, leaving our family alone in the gathering autumn dusk, we approached the coffin and wrote our own messages, words of hope, truth and love that only the Bible offers.

I resisted leaving for as long as I could, but the grave workers were waiting and a golden fall sunset was already dimming through the leafless trees to the west. To me, it felt like the second time I was leaving my boy cold and alone on the ground.

In his first talk with us the day after we received the news about Paul, Pastor Ross had prepared us that the day after the funeral is Day One of the grief journey. It was indeed true for my husband who had faithfully dealt, over the past two weeks, not only with Paul's final paycheque and bank account, death certificate, insurance claims, funeral arrangements and legal matters, but also with frequent police and victim services updates. Exhausted, he soon withdrew from the group that gathered back at the church for a meal, to spend time alone and weep.

Chapter 20 – A Defense of Punk

"I wanted you to know that my heart has been heavy for you all," wrote a girl from the Red Deer punk community shortly after the funeral. "Paul was an amazing kid with the ability to impact people in a large way in a short time. I feel truly blessed to have spent some time getting to know him in the last few months. I expected and wish for more time with him."

I thanked the girl who sent this message and, knowing she had been at the band venue the night Paul died, I told her I'd like to talk.

"Right now," I wrote in response, "all the punk stuff I read and see on the Facebook page and on Paul's own page is like blow after blow, so painful. All those images of violence and death." I added that we were supported by the love of God and his people through that time.

As I write this now, years later, I notice elements once considered uniquely punk have now become mainstream. I frequently see toddlers sporting mohawks and older women tattooed or with streaks of blue or green in their hair. With normalization comes loss of impact and meaning. It takes more and more outrageous images and ideas to get attention in a culture immune to shock. The punk look has begun to seem tame, but at the time, it still had shock value.

> *I'm glad you have the support of family,"* the girl messaged in return. *"I know the church is behind you a hundred percent too and your whole community. I'm sorry to hear that you're finding some of the Facebook posts upsetting. The community of people you see on there is full of love. But I hear that the imagery is difficult and probably confusing. I know my own parents have struggled to understand my lifestyle too, and I understand why. It can all seem dark sometimes. I wish I could help you guys see it all differently. Maybe someday I can.*
>
> *What I know is that Paul was happy and sweet and truly innocent! I also know that the punk community, which is a family of its own, is rallying to offer support up here. You'd be amazed to speak to some of these people, to hear the positive effect Paul had on them, myself included. They are all thinking of you: sending their thoughts, their prayers, their energies, their own versions of support. Please know that no one's intentions are bad; what they see and say on there is just a different language of love. Very different. The imagery is dark, but it's not meant to harm or hurt. I thought for a long time about what I could or should say to you. There isn't really anything to say, I guess, but I hope you can find some comfort in knowing everyone's positive intentions.*

It was kind of this girl to extend condolences and try to explain the violent imagery, foul-language, anger and hate. I did, in fact, understand that no one's intentions were bad; that no one meant to harm or hurt. But to us it was hurtful. It only added to our grief. Why did young people just like Paul see the tragedy of the actual flesh-and-blood death of one of their peers yet fail to recognize the death-celebrating worldview they embraced? To "help us see it all differently" seemed a little like "helping" someone understand that throwing rotten tomatoes at their face is just my way of showing love to them. There was a cultural communication barrier.

The idea, too, that the punk community was a family of its own was a painful blow in itself. I'd read how young men without fathers or from dysfunctional families gravitate toward gangs as a substitute for what they've missed at home. It added to my sense of failure that Paul found the need to search for another, better family.

While these well-meant words and messages and shared songs hurt, reminders of Jesus' attitude toward those who misunderstood him kept returning to me. "Bless them, forgive them," he said. I prayed for the strength to do so.

A couple of weeks later, the girl sent another message. "Hello Eleanor, I hope the last few weeks have gone smoothly for you. I'm still thinking of you and your family often. I wanted you to know that as these weeks become quieter, my thoughts and prayers are still with you."

I thanked her for her ongoing thoughtfulness throughout the time of our sorrow. But increasingly, my conscience was bothered by something I'd said the last time I'd spoken to her in person.

"I regret one thing I said to you at the funeral – that punk 'killed my kid.' Of course, it's not true, any more than the idea that punk is keeping my other kids alive. But early on, I had such a feeling of despair, knowing that Paul was so devoted to a subculture that is obsessed with the exact opposite of what Jesus offers and what we tried to teach him – truth, joy, peace, love, life! So, when I see others glorifying him, claiming him for their own as some kind of martyr for the punk cause, when in fact, he deeply hurt us and others who loved him as he selfishly pursued his own thing through the past year and a half, I am truly grieved. I do understand that the punk kids at the funeral and those who write on the Facebook page are well-meaning. I just wish they would get the connection that that whole subculture is truly a dead end. I'm sure some of them have parents grieving over them and praying for them too and I feel for those parents."

To their credit, and despite appearances and bad language, the young people of the punk "family" held a benefit concert a few weeks later and presented us with a generous fund toward funeral expenses. I was torn between frustration at the inconsistency of their cause and tender gratitude. The memory of the Good Samaritan punk in the drama of my college days returned to me. I had been judging by outward appearance only. For all the harsh and coarse rudeness of their culture, clearly these kids genuinely cared for Paul and for us.

Chapter 21 – Road to Repentance

Long before the flower arrangements had withered and the donated casseroles and plates of cookies were gone, the last of our family members left for home. Now a new normal life had to resume. Among the many condolence cards gathered in a basket at the funeral had been a book offered by a friend. *Where Does a Mother Go to Resign?* is the story of how the author, Barbara Johnson, faced her son's homosexuality and his disappearance into the gay lifestyle for over eleven years. *Did someone think this was the situation with our son?* I was a little disturbed to be offered such a book, but soon I saw it also chronicled the early deaths of two of Johnson's other sons.

I could relate so completely to her description of life in a dark valley of depression, secluding herself in her home in shame. After many months, Johnson reached out and wrote to Dr. Walter Martin, founder of the Christian Research Institute and the original host of the Bible Answer Man radio program. Though my circumstances were different, I was as hungry for hope as she was. Surely someone so knowledgeable in the scriptures would be able to offer insights I hadn't yet considered.

Can we hope for the prodigal son's return, Johnson wanted to know? Martin answered this way:

> *If the child belongs to God, God will bring him to repentance … this is a cosmic law: no one, no how, can get away with nuthin'! Our young friend may think he can; but somewhere down the line when he is trying hard to forget all about it, God is going to get his attention. The Lord told Israel that it's sudden when it comes upon you and you don't know it. He says, "I will remember you." He is remembering His prodigal son. God will always have the last word. He tells you what you should do – and then He graciously hounds you until you say, "Yes, Lord!"*

God has promised, "I Myself will search for My sheep and seek them out. I will seek what was lost and bring back what was driven away" (Ezekiel 34: 11, 15). This was all fine for her son who was still living, but what about mine, now dead?

I knew from I Corinthians 11:30 that God, at times, disciplines believers by allowing them to become sick or even die if they glibly partook of the Lord's Supper (Communion) yet actively destroyed the unity of believers. And even though Ananias and Sapphira were numbered with the believers in the early church, yet for their lying they were killed by God as a warning to the entire church. There is nothing in the text to say they went to hell, only that their physical bodies died.

The death of believers is not to be considered a punishment for sin, writes theologian Wayne Grudem. "Even the death of some Corinthian Christians who had been abusing the Lord's Supper is viewed by [the apostle] Paul as a disciplining or chastening process, not as a result of condemnation."

But our son Paul had never taken Communion. As far as I knew, other than the somewhat dubious profession of faith he made to the lady who wrote me the letter, there was little, if any, evidence that in life, Paul was a Christian. In fact, just four months earlier, when his youth pastor had asked our son where he would spend eternity if he were to die that day, Paul had answered, "Probably in hell." By his own evaluation, he thought he deserved hell. At least he had a right appraisal of what our sin earns each one of us.

"All who wander are not lost," someone quoted, trying to comfort me in my confusion about Paul's eternal state. Although I wanted to believe this, it appeared to support a kind of universal salvation, saying anyone who is wandering away from God and his truth would still go to heaven. That could apply to every human being who ever lived. I knew universalism wasn't taught in scripture. Later I discovered the actual quote from a poem by J.R.R. Tolkien read, "Not all those who wander are lost." This was indeed a comfort. In fact, the truth of it resonated with me, since we are all "prone to wander," as the old hymn says. Does a day go by in which any of us has not drifted in our focus on God or our love and trust in him? If Paul had belonged to God, there was certainly hope I would meet him again one day. *But had he?* Not knowing Paul's spiritual condition was by far the most painful thing about losing him.

It led to an inevitable question. Was there any evidence in scripture to support the idea that God might purposely bring an unbeliever close to death in order to bring him to repentance? The seed of this idea must have been planted by reading I had done just two weeks prior to Paul's death. I'd bought *Crowded to Christ* by L.E. Maxwell at a used book sale. The author emphasizes God's use of the "mounting miseries" of life to edge people ever closer to Christ. "There are things worse than trouble," Maxwell wrote, "worse than pain, worse than death. Sin, to God, is the only unendurable." And God's promise in Psalm 50:15 confirmed it. "Call upon Me in the day of trouble; I will deliver you and you shall glorify Me."

It seemed the answer was yes. The thief crucified on the cross next to Christ was the clearest example of a dying person receiving salvation. But that criminal had been consciously able to profess his belief and trust in Jesus. Paul's final moments of unconsciousness remained a barrier to this kind of last-minute conversion. At least for me. Then I recalled my neighbor Rosanna's nephew describing things he'd experienced during the time he'd been in a coma. It seemed an indication his mind and spirit were active even while his body wasn't. Could it be that unconsciousness was no barrier at all to an all-powerful God? What it came down to was the question: How merciful is God?

Our pastor had quoted II Peter 3:9 to me, reminding me that the Lord is "longsuffering toward us, not willing that any should perish but that all should come to repentance." But I found the verse confusing. I knew that *not* everyone repents and many do perish eternally. Did it mean, then, that God was unable to do anything about this? Instinctively I recoiled from the image of such a weak and helpless God. The meaning of that critical word "all" became clearer when I studied the context. The Apostle was writing to believers, explaining that though people may scoff, God's judgment will assuredly come. When Peter says God is longsuffering toward *us* (believers), it's to explain that God is holding off his judgment on evil, in order to bring all his own people to repentance. I began to see the focus here was on repentance. How merciful is God? God is putting up with a whole lot of evil so he can bring glory to himself by making believers out of sinners! "In

His forbearance God had passed over the sins that were previously committed, to demonstrate at the present time His righteousness, that He might be just and the justifier of the one who has faith in Jesus" (Romans 3: 25b, 26). And he'll hold back his judgment until the full contingent of worshippers is safely in the fold.

Chapter 22 – A Valley of Prayer

Early in 2012, I had feared my prayers for my children might not be answered. Now it was an urgent question, *Were they?* How could I know if God had answered my prayers for Paul?

My walk through a dark valley of shadow had begun the year before in January of 2011. A few months earlier, two of our sons had moved out, leaving only Paul and our youngest, Timothy, at home. At the time, I was unaware what a critical change that was for Paul. Because we'd always home-schooled, he'd just lost his lifelong peer group – his best buddies. He must have felt abandoned and alone.

Although I had misgivings about the boys' leaving, I distinctly remember a feeling of satisfaction and well-being. Life is good, I thought. We had a good relationship with each of our children. Five of them had reached adulthood and they seemed comfortable identifying with a Christian way of life. Many behaviours and habits that were a result of peer-pressure, tended to be strongest in the teen years and the oldest five were now out of their teens, without adopting those behaviours. Surely their good example would have a trickle-down effect on the youngest as well. I felt secure, confident that none of them would ever be involved in promiscuous sex or drug or alcohol abuse. But can we ever know what lies ahead?

The first inkling I had that things were not well with some of my sons was a Facebook image of one of them getting a tattoo. I could scarcely believe it. They were always up to some crazy staging of photos and videos, from "drinking" farm herbicide to creating an "earthworm burger" (in my kitchen!). Those shenanigans I had found amusing. Surely this was just another of these fakes. But further Facebook revelations followed. Then came the piercings. And the posting of pictures and links sympathizing with immorality. It got to the point that I dreaded checking social media. Fear and worry became my constant grim companions.

My thought life began to take a downward spiral. I examined everything I'd done and taught our children through the years, doubting I'd taught it well, doubting it was enough. All I could see was my failures. Soon, everything in life seemed black and hopeless. I believed the most important roles in my life – my marriage, mothering, home-educating – had been a pitiful wash-out. Craving affirmation and reassurance in all my relationships, when I received it, I didn't believe it. When someone made a suggestion for improvement, I saw criticism. When they expressed displeasure, I heard faultfinding. Silence, I understood as hostility.

This was not what would have been considered clinical depression. It was not the kind of depression I'd seen years before in a close friend, where personal hygiene deteriorated and she was nearly unable to get out of bed in the morning. I was still able to function in my daily education and housekeeping responsibilities. But they became chores bereft of the joy I'd usually found in them.

It was a vortex that all too soon sucked me down into a deep pit of darkness.

One thing kept me from utter despair. Prayer. Prayer is a line of two-way communication between me, a creature, and my Creator. It's an astounding privilege to freely, directly speak to the God of the universe and have him respond through his written word. Even when my soul-anguish choked off words, I had the assurance that God's Spirit took over for me. What I was to discover was that more than achieving my list of demands, it changes my heart, inclining me to want what God wants.

One day I was lamenting to my sister my frequent doubts that God would answer my prayers. How I wished that no matter what, I could sail through life unperturbed, with complete confidence that everything would work out well.

"There's this constant back-and-forth inside me," I told her. "I'll have a sudden fear of some dire outcome in the lives of the boys, and then a scripture will come to mind answering it. But next thing I know, another fear pops up."

"Did it ever occur to you that it's the Holy Spirit who is using God's Word to keep giving you faith?" she asked. It hadn't occurred to me.

What an encouragement to know that God was actively at work in me, like a guardrail keeping me from tumbling over the edge of despair. Doubts came, but Truth nailed them! Some of the most tattered, tear-stained pages of my Bible contain God's precious promises.

> *"All your children shall be taught by the Lord, And great shall be the peace of your children. (Isaiah 54:13)*

> *"Thus says the Lord: 'Refrain your voice from weeping, And your eyes from tears; For your work shall be rewarded, says the Lord, And they shall come back from the land of the enemy. There is hope in your future, says the Lord, That your children shall come back to their own border." (Jeremiah 31:16, 17)*

I saw from the Bible that God loves his straying, sinning people far more than any mother ever loves her child. He speaks of Israel (Ephraim) as "My dear son… a pleasant child." He says he earnestly remembers his son.

"Therefore My heart yearns for him; I will surely have mercy on him, says the Lord." (Jeremiah 31:20)

I applied God's yearning first to my own soul and then to my sons as God's beloved, though rebellious, children.

Another help in fighting bleak thoughts was to sing my way through a hymnbook, particularly songs of praise to God for who he is – his power and love. One hymn that became my go-to for staving off the downward thought spiral was Isaac Watts' *O God Our Help in Ages Past.*

O God our help in ages past,
Our hope for years to come,
Our shelter from the stormy blast,
And our eternal home!

Under the shadow of Thy throne,
Still may we dwell secure.
Sufficient is Thine arm alone
And our defense is sure.

I'd seen God's help in the past "ages" of my own life.

Again and again, he had provided for our many financial and physical needs through the years. His answers to our prayers for our older children gave me hope that he would continue to do so for years to come. And I knew that he is the only shelter from the temptation to give up hope. That hymn was my constant refrain during those months.

Back to Prayer. Throughout that year and a half of emotional darkness my mother would often remind me that worry is a sin. It's really a belief that God is not powerful enough to solve the problem or that he doesn't care. Both are faulty thinking. Weakly, I began to catch my fear, worry and self-recrimination before they spiraled downward, by directing these thoughts to prayer.

In the same way I used to see pregnant women everywhere upon learning I was expecting, now I learned of other parents suffering under the burden of straying children. More and more I heard of young people whose Christian parents were in anguish over their children's rejection of the God they'd been raised to love.

A thought entered my mind, are you the only one with this problem? I sensed God prompting me to pray faithfully for other prodigals and their parents. But at first, I closed my ears, consumed by my own problems. Such is the selfishness of worry. In some twisted way, it seemed if I included these others in my prayers my own concerns would be diluted. Uh… yeah, that was exactly God's point.

Gradually I added thirty names to my prodigals list. Young and old, known to me or unknown. Some had been estranged from their parents for many years while others were in harmony with their parents but not with God. Some were living a delinquent life, others lived respectably, yet with hearts far from God. Whether I was in regular contact with those parents or not, I prayed faithfully for these names along with my own sons. It did not take away my personal concerns, but it redirected my worries into faith.

After months of feeling a heavy burden, almost a desperation to pray, and the accumulation of bleak blackness in my outlook, I reached a breaking point. One Sunday afternoon in June, fed up with a silent, unappreciative household, I drove off not knowing, or caring, where I was going.

Alone with my Bible on the pier of a lakeshore miles from home, I poured out my heart to the Lord. I reminded him of his promises – that he loved my sons far more even than I did. That he is all powerful and can overrule even a willful human heart, giving it the very desire for God. And that his Holy Spirit could use means of which I was completely unaware.

"I know you're at work even when I can't see it," I cried out to him. *But I want to* **see** *something! Do something Lord!* Spent from sobbing, I was soothed by the sun on my back and the lap of water against the wooden pier where I sat.

It was time to go home. Though nothing had changed, God and I were at peace. I would trust him, even if it took decades. The question came to mind, even if the answer never comes in your lifetime? I hesitated… Yes, even then.

On the way home, I stopped in to drop off something for our son living in town. I watched him muscle the small bookcase into his apartment. Before I left, he said, "Guess who was in church today."

The story he told me was surprising. A couple whose rocky marriage had ended in divorce a year earlier had been in church together that day. I had previously prayed for them and was grieved when I heard of the split. But I hadn't continued to pray. Now here they were, hard hearts softened, working toward reconciliation. Oh, me of little faith! The impact of this improbable, late and astonishing answer to requests I had made of God years before, was powerful. He did answer! He wasn't hampered by hard hearts! He could overturn circumstances that seemed impossible!

Chapter 23 – Means and Ends

The following week, I noticed a lightness within, a growing optimism. Not even Paul's looming English 30 final exam and his frustrating lack of concern to study for it could dampen my raised spirits. *Should I have bothered seeing the doctor last week to have my hormone levels checked?* It hadn't occurred to me to do so when I first began the plunge into depression because I had no other symptoms. Since I was "of a certain age," I had finally admitted there could be an organic cause for my long-term angst. Yet like a watched pot that never boils, my depression now seemed to have lifted.

It must be the eager anticipation of Becky and the twins arriving on Saturday, I thought. *It'll be back to the pit once they leave.* But for now, my head was full of plans and preparations for our daughter's and granddaughters' coming visit, a welcome change. I decided to enjoy the freedom from misery. One day at a time.

And it was a wonderful time! Nothing can warm a discouraged grandmother's heart like the spontaneous, soft-armed hugs of a loving child. Nothing can drag a self-absorbed teen out of himself like the wistful brown eyes of a pair of nieces. I wish I had a photo of the memory in my mind – Paul in his white T-shirt with the sleeves cut off, holding hands with the two-year-old twins and taking them outside to play on the swings. His obvious joy in doing it spoke to me, softening my heart toward him.

I was sad to see them leave for more reasons than the sorrow of parting. I feared that inevitable return to the Slough of Despond. But the darkness did not return. I had enthusiasm for projects once again. I organized the garage. We painted the outside of it and not even Paul's sullen disinterest in helping – "Why should I care what colour the garage is?" – dimmed my energy. We built shelves to line the garage walls and I painted them. I sorted and overhauled belongings in one of our outbuildings. I finally had energy and motivation to create the concrete cobblestone pathway in the area where Paul had prepared the ground.

When I returned to the doctor for a follow-up a week later, he pronounced all my levels good.

"You're a little low on vitamin D, so you could probably triple or quadruple what you're taking but it won't begin to make a difference for about six months."

So, the black cloud had no physical cause. And its departure had nothing to do with any supplements I was taking. Whatever the case, I was simply glad to be free of it. Paul's silence remained, I still had to prod him to study for exams, the marks he'd already received were a disappointment, but my outlook remained sunny.

I relate all this to show that the eighteen months of walking through a dark valley were not hormone-related. I believe the pressing, weighty burden to pray, the near-desperation I experienced during that time were a God-initiated call to prayer.

The Westminster Confession of Faith tells us, "God, from all eternity, did by the most wise and holy counsel of his own will, freely and unchangeably ordain whatsoever comes to pass." In the past, it had made me wonder, if God has decided everything that happens beforehand, why pray? But the same question arises in the opposite scenario. If everything is up to human will or random chance, why pray?

"God does hear our prayers," writes blogger Jim Elliff, in an article on "Comfort for Christian Parents of Unconverted Children." "Though God has taught us that He chooses all who are His before the foundation of the world, He also taught us that we should pray, and not only pray, but expect the answer to our prayers. It is true that God is sovereign and it is just as true that He answers prayer. In fact, He could not answer prayer if He were not in control of all things."

Again, the Confession teaches that "God ordains the means as well as the ends." In other words, God has designed both the *ways* things he wants to happen will come to pass, as well as the *end results* themselves. If his plan is to adopt a person as his own child, he plans and ensures the method by which it will happen.

What are some of those methods? Preaching, evangelism, and prayer. God likes to have us involved in his work. In fact, that's how he has chosen to accomplish it. When we pray for something consistent with what he has planned, it's because he has prompted us to do so. Years earlier, I had begun the practice of immediately praying for a person whose name would suddenly spring up in my memory, though I may not have thought of them for many years. I believed those random thoughts were not random at all but were a prayer-prompt from God for his purposes. I want to be clear when I speak of prayer-prompts. I'm not claiming special revelation from God, or special knowledge of how or when that prayer will be answered. Nor do I have a license to formulate theology in any way I please. Rather, inner nudges and promptings are part of the dynamic relationship with the living God that is available to anyone who believes.

"A true burden in prayer for your child," Elliff writes, "is a gift from God. A persistent burden may indicate that God intends to give your child eternal life because authentic prayer always begins with God. Though we cannot be absolutely certain that we know all that God is doing, we should be optimistic if the burden continues."

Others too, I was to learn, had experienced God's inexplicable promptings to pray. Vicky, the friend who earlier had written the letter about Paul, shared her story with me:

> *Next to my grandma, my dad was the most important person in my life. When I was told that his body was shutting down, it became a burden to pray for his salvation. I was actually praying for recovery as well because I held on to his invincibility. He was my dad, after all!*
>
> *I prayed frequently throughout the days for him, but when I was told it was only a matter of time, I finally understood what a "burden" prayer could be: I prayed for him almost continually throughout the day. It was an unproductive day. I only stopped praying when it became too sad. When I was ready to control my emotions, I started praying again. I hardly ate. It wasn't intentional — I had no appetite. I couldn't sleep, so I lay there praying into the wee hours. But of course, I did fall asleep because all of a sudden, I woke up, wide awake, to a voice saying, "Help me!" It wasn't an audible voice. More like words. It was so startling I just lay there for a second, wondering where it came from. It only took another second to remember the reason for my 24/7 burden — it was my dad! Somehow, I knew he*

was dying, and probably scared. He wouldn't be asking for help otherwise.

So, at 5:17 in the morning (according to my bedside radio-alarm), I prayed the same thing over and over, "Father, please help my dad! Please take his hand and lead him home! Please help him find Jesus and take his hand so he can go home. Father, please help my dad!"

Three minutes later, at 5:20 a.m. (MST), I sensed another "voice" saying, "You can stop now!" It was as abrupt as the first "voice" and although it didn't include a confirmation of salvation, I believed my dad was in heaven.

After a couple of months, I called the hospice to inquire about the time of death. It was 7:20 EST, 5:20 MST. How much more confirmation did I need? Why else, when I was so exhausted from praying, would I have woken up with such a start — three minutes before his death — to a voice directly related to my intense, fervent, single-minded prayers. There is no other explanation for me than believing that God wanted me to witness my dad's salvation. And I will always be thankful for that!

That summer of 2012, I experienced three months of freedom from the heaviness of fear and worry that I previously had been redirecting into prayer. Returning to my normal level of busyness in life, I confess I missed the sense of nearness to God that I'd had while in the dark valley. Oh, I still read the Bible and prayed. But the fervency and urgency were gone.

Weeks after Paul's death, still barely grasping the finality of it, I was floundering in the quagmire of questions about where he was. It was bitter to know that both my husband and I had soundly slept through the events that killed our son. He lay cold and hurt and dying on a distant city street while we were safe at home in bed. Many times before, when our other sons were out beyond our control and care, God had awakened me with an urgent sense that I was to pray for them. I had always felt honoured to be included in God's protection and restraint of our boys through prayer. Why not this time when the need was clearly so vital?

I was *not* prodded awake to pray on the night of October 5-6, 2012. Would there have been anything to accomplish by doing so? It was God's appointed time for Paul's life to end.

> *"To everything there is a season,*
> *A time for every purpose under heaven:*
> *A time to be born*
> *And a time to die..." (Ecclesiastes 3:1,2)*

> *"Your eyes saw my substance, being yet unformed,*
> *And in Your book they all were written,*
> *The days fashioned for me,*
> *When as yet there were none of them." (Psalm 139:16)*

This one hard-to-swallow fact helped me accept the biblical teaching that what happened to Paul was not an accident. Oh yes, humanly speaking, the collision did not seem to be intentional. But more importantly, in the bigger picture from God's point of view, it was an event ordained by God. He does not *cause* evil or suffering, but for his good purposes he permits it, limits it, and uses those who cause it.

Do I like that? Of course not. I don't understand it. Paul's life seems unfinished to me. But I trust the kind of God that would enter into the world he created and pour out his life for the very ones who have messed up that perfect creation and rejected him.

Discovering that God ordains the means as well as the ends gave me a genuine hope that my prayers for Paul were answered. As created beings, we can't be entirely sure he answers our prayers in the way we ask because "the secret things belong to the Lord our God" (Deuteronomy 29:29). Yet while there is mystery in the way God works, I believe he ordained my valley of prayer. If so, there was a very real possibility that Paul's ultimate salvation was also the desired end — his plan! This, at last, was something firm to grip in the fog of questions about Paul's eternal destiny. And in the time after his funeral, grasping this theological truth, a flame flared and caught inside me. It lit the way for hope.

Chapter 24 – Life Before Death

October 22, 2012: One week to the day since we buried our son. I'm starting my day with a tall glass of water and my Bible. Throughout the year, the Bible study guide I use has been following and explaining the biblical basis for the 1563 Heidelberg Catechism. Early in the year, I'd found its opening question and answer brimming with comfort and solace.

> *Q. What is your only comfort in life and death?*
>
> *A. That I am not my own, but belong – body and soul, in life and death – to my faithful Saviour Jesus Christ. He fully paid for all my sins with His precious blood, and set me free from all the tyranny of the devil. He also watches over me in such a way that not a hair can fall from my head without the will of my Father in heaven.*

But I shy away from the title of today's entry. Stark and startling, it reads, "God's Furious Anger." Shaken, I hesitate. *Do I want to read this at a time when I already feel soul-singed by God's wrath?* I read on.

> *The idea of God's anger and wrath is not popular in many circles today. Critics, however, fail to understand that the Lord could not be meaningfully righteous, good, holy, or merciful if He did not pour out His wrath on evil. A good being hates what is evil...God is never sadistic, tired, or irritable. He is not a short-tempered hothead. Since He is perfectly righteous, His anger is always righteous and good (Ps. 97:6).*

There's more but I'm already inwardly trembling. I'm comforted by the reminder at the bottom of the page that if God has brought me into a saving relationship with Jesus I never need to fear his wrath again. But that's for me. I'm desperate for reassurance about Paul.

As I usually do, I look up the scriptures listed for further study. The first reference, Proverbs 11:23, warns me that the "expectation of the wicked is wrath." That's harrowing for me to contemplate today.

Quickly, I leaf over to the next passage. Hosea 11:8, 9. Already I anticipate the book's intimate portrayal of God's loving longing for his unfaithful people, like a husband pursuing a disloyal wife or a parent pursuing a straying child. *But will there be something in it for my grieving heart?*

> *"How can I give you up, Ephraim?*
> *How can I hand you over, Israel?*

Okay, I gather this is God talking here. Ephraim and Israel are terms for God's covenant people. I hear the longing in his voice. The verse ahead of this one describes God's people as "bent on backsliding from" him. I can't help but see the parallel between these folks and Paul. He certainly seemed to be bent on backsliding from God.

> *How can I make you like Admah?*
> *How can I set you like Zeboiim?*

I stop to look up those A to Z names. They're towns that were destroyed along with God's judgment on Sodom and Gomorrah back in Genesis.

My heart churns within Me; my sympathy is stirred.

God's emotion here jumps out at me. He doesn't want to destroy his erring people. his great heart of love is far more inclined to mercy for his beloved people than to destruction. I read on, my own heart beating faster.

> *I will not execute the fierceness of My anger;*
> *I will not again destroy Ephraim.*

It's like God is resolving not to give them what they deserve. God's desire to extend mercy triumphs over the judgment they deserve.

> *For I am God, and not man,*

Humans faced with the animosity and rejection God experiences from his creatures would, without a doubt, return the same kind of treatment. God's not like us. I'm reminded of the verse in Romans that says, "While we were still sinners, Christ died for us."

> *The Holy One in your midst;*

And I will not come with terror.

But Lord, it seems You did come with terror! By now I'm personalizing the passage.

They shall walk after the Lord.
He will roar like a lion.

Oh yes, Lord, you've roared! I'm deafened and trembling with your roaring! But I don't see the difference between the "coming with terror" you said you wouldn't do, and the roaring the next line here assures me you will do. I look up other passages about roaring. And I find in Isaiah 31 a description of God as a lion, roaring to defend, deliver and preserve his people. Obviously, God thinks differently than we do. "Roaring" is a warning of imminent destruction. Was the collision that crushed Paul yet another of God's dire warnings to call a rebel to repent?

When He roars,

It's a certainty. God is going to respond in judgment.

Then His sons shall come trembling from the west.

A son comes trembling from the west! Seriously? My body tenses, gripped with what I see at first as a significant coincidence. Our son was killed an hour west of home. But no, that's not how to understand scripture. The biblical "west" means Egypt, a reference to ancient Israel's habit of running off to Egypt or false gods whenever they were in trouble – anything instead of trusting God to help them.

But the word "trembling?" I read this line over and over hardly daring to hope. I must be sure of the proper interpretation. Eagerly I check cross-references and flip pages to Isaiah 66:2.

> *But on this one will I look; On him who is poor and of a contrite spirit, And who trembles at My word.*

Trembling is a synonym for fearing the Lord! Gradually, light and truth pierce through my foggy grief. The point of the passage is that God's judgment may hurt his people, but he does it to bring them to repentance.

Again, I read the line: "*His sons* **shall come** *trembling.*"

The definite certainty of it! When God acts, even his straying chosen ones repent! He makes it happen! "He **will** save His people from their sins." (Matthew 1:21) Paul's eternal destiny was not dependent solely on his own decisions. As it is for all of us, it was dependent on God putting a spark of life into his dead spirit and making him willing to repent!

> *But God, who is rich in mercy, because of His great love with which He loved us, even when we were dead in trespasses,* **made us alive** *together with Christ (by grace you have been saved). (Ephesians 2:4,5)*

For the first time since that early morning visit from the police three weeks before, I felt my soul land on stable ground. Finally, I had something tangible, a firm foundation for my hope. People's well-meant comments that Paul was "a good kid" had been nice but unconvincing. My "vision" of Paul looking happy and seeming to speak to me about heaven was too subjective, too easily explained away considering my own overwrought emotions.

But this passage was solid, based as it was on the character of God. God is overwhelmingly gracious and merciful to his children. He warns them and calls them back to himself when they stray. And he yearns to forgive them. While it was written *to* the people of Israel, it was written *for* all people everywhere in every generation, including me.

In the weeks and months following, I continued to find passages showing God roaring in warning of judgment, with the intention of drawing rebels back to himself. He warns rebellious people of coming disaster, then foretells their return to him in loving reunion.

> *"Is Ephraim My dear son?...For though I spoke against him, I earnestly remember him still. Therefore My heart yearns for him. I will surely have mercy on him, says the Lord." (Jeremiah 31:20)*

> *"And the Lord will strike and heal ... they will return to the Lord and He will be entreated by them and heal them." (Isaiah 19:22)*

> *"You have received gifts among men, Even from the rebellious, That the Lord might dwell there." (Psalm 66:18)*

It wasn't the definitive, absolute assurance I craved, but it was enough for me. I could trust God with Paul's eternal destiny because I could rely on the character and nature of God. It was that big, conditional and terrifying ***if*** that had so shaken me when my husband had said if Paul was one of God's chosen ones, he would not have failed to save him. And I was shaken because I was viewing things from my human vantage point. Now, God had shown me a glimpse of what he is like. How does he treat his people? He is exponentially more loving and merciful than we are. I could rest in who God is.

Chapter 25 –Love, Your Son

Author Danielle Steele, whose son Nick Traina took his own life at age nineteen, records excerpts from the journal he kept at age fourteen. "I have irrepressible feelings about my mother," he wrote. "I love her so much it hurts. I tell her but I don't know if she knows it for real… When I tell her, it feels really good that I'd told her, but then if I do something that inadvertently or even purposely hurts her, I feel like I've disproved myself."

I, by contrast, have so few indications of any affection or love Paul had for me to counterbalance the daily eye-rolling disgust he exhibited. I don't even have any notes or letters signed, "Love, Paul." Did Paul love me? His dad? His family?

These questions gnawed at me deeply, given the strain we lived with during the years while he was at home as a teen. On one occasion, I asked him when he thought the tension between us had started. He shocked me by saying, "when I was 12." I had thought it was more like the past two or three years.

I cling to the long-ago memory of his huge, dark baby-eyes gazing intently into my face.

Another memory haunts me with regret. Our oldest was finally old enough to be left in charge of the younger children and I was finding a new freedom to run errands without packing up six youngsters to take with me. One day, I needed to run to the bank and two other brief stops and was just pulling away from the house when I saw 18-month old Paul watching me leave. He stood at the screen door, gripping the glass, frantically crying. At the time, my feelings of guilt at abandoning him were easily set aside with the knowledge that I'd be back within an hour, and that it wouldn't be any fun for him anyway. But with the perspective of his death, the simple memory took on a new and bitter significance, opening a whole new cavern of sorrow and remorse. Still, it is evidence that like any young child, Paul was bonded to his mother.

I have the memory of his return from his first-ever month away from home on a mission trip. He flew the last leg of the homeward journey with his cousin to Manitoba where we met him at my brother's farm. By the time my husband, Timo and I arrived, Paul had been there for a day. And while the rest of the relatives were indoors when we drove in the yard, there was Paul, outside in the summer sunshine, waiting for us. Though he didn't say so, he seemed eager and happy to see us.

Because of Paul's willing sacrifice, I have a sewing room. Two years before his passing, Paul moved into an empty bedroom so he wouldn't have to share with his younger brother. But I had ear-marked it for a sewing room. When I asked if he'd be willing to move to an unfinished space in the basement, he gave up the room without complaint and moved his belongings downstairs.

I have the proof that he viewed his home and parents as a haven and source of help by bringing his girlfriend home when he didn't know how to help her.

Another incident has changed from a bitter memory to a positive one. In one of our talks with him about the direction his life was taking, he complained, "You're always ganging up on me." At the time, his words made me feel like giving up. I'd heard parenting experts emphasize the importance of presenting a united front to our children, that division was confusing and unsettling to kids. Now Paul found fault even with that. But with the perspective of time, I've come to see Paul's complaint as a back-handed compliment. Staying together, united in our parenting was one thing we did right for him, even though he never lived to learn to appreciate it.

I have the empty box from the only gift he ever gave me – the Valentine's chocolates he bought and presented to me.

And I have the tightening of Paul's arms around me when I gave him a hug the last time I saw him at his dad's birthday celebration the weekend before his death.

It's just not enough.

Sorrow overwhelms me when I think of the many life joys Paul missed by dying in his teens. He never knew the thrill of independence that comes with buying his own car, or even his own phone. He never went to college, slogging through pressures to achieve something even more valuable than the degree – perseverance. He never experienced the delight of lifelong oneness with a beloved wife; nor the joy and intimacy of sexual ecstasy. He never thrilled to the cozy heft of his own newborn child in his arms, the marvel of his own flesh and blood. He never traveled the world, celebrated Communion, read a thousand wonderful books, watched his child grow up. He also never endured a dental filling, failed a course, lost a job, experienced the death of a loved one, contracted a terminal disease, grew feeble and old.

If I thought, as some do, that this life is all there is – that we live a few years, reproduce and ultimately become compost – I would certainly despair. The joys of life I listed, those markers of independence, fulfillment and success in life, quickly pale when we're faced with pain and loss and suffering. That's because life's highs are mere shadows of the ultimate reality they represent. What the hungry human heart really wants is belonging, coming home to the one who knows us through and through and loves us anyway. We crave truth, beauty and love, but we substitute false satisfactions for the God who alone offers what we need.

Assuming Paul is with the Lord, would I wish Paul back, if it were in my power? I thought hard about that in the weeks ahead of his brother's wedding a year and a half after Paul's death. It was the first time we would be together as a family since Paul's funeral and I desperately longed for an updated family photo – without gaps! I caught myself wishing, *if only he could come back, even just for pictures!* But it doesn't work that way. If he returned from the dead, we would want him with us always. Going through the loss a second time was unthinkable!

And when I imagined it from Paul's perspective, I knew I couldn't wish on him a return to this life. Force him back from endless bliss to this veil of tears? "How wicked it would be, if we could, to call the dead back!" wrote C.S. Lewis when he found himself wondering the same thing after the loss of his beloved wife, Joy.

Jesus corrected those who did not believe in the resurrection of the dead. "But concerning the dead, that they rise, have you not read in the book of Moses, in the burning bush passage, how God spoke to him, saying, 'I am the God of Abraham, the God of Isaac, and the God of Jacob'? He is not the God of the dead, but the God of the living." (Mark 12:26, 27) Here Jesus referred to men who had died many centuries before, as *living*. To live is to think and feel, to consciously experience life, to relate to other people and to God.

We can be sure Paul would have a very different perspective on his life now. Nothing of value can be lost in death; not our humanity or personality, not enjoyment of life, not the bonds of relationships with loved ones and certainly not worship or love for God and his Word. The way our human nature reflects God – creativity, friendship, memories, everything that makes us human – transcends the physical death of our bodies and lasts for eternity. Only losing sight of that profound weight of glory makes me, selfish and small-minded, want my son back with us.

While nothing of value is lost through death, everything that makes life in this world miserable, is. Paul wouldn't be missing this life. Sorrow and loss, death and disease, goodbyes and evil, disappointment and doubt – it's all wiped away in the moment of supreme lucidity when we see Christ. And the most debilitating thing we shed when we die is our cursed tendency toward sin. The Heidelberg catechism calls death "an end to sinning and the door to eternal life." I can only imagine the wonder of being enveloped in the rapturous love of God, my every thought and motive pure, unselfish and free at last from pervasive insidious sin! How could I want anything less for Paul?

Chapter 26 – Training for What?

A thick blanket of snow covered Paul's grave, the cemetery, and our world the week after the funeral. It stayed, growing thicker in the months that followed, muffling sound outside and feeling inside me. As true Canadians, we'd always been cheered at the smallest signs of spring thaw. But that winter, as March gave way to April, my husband and I both dreaded the appearance of spring. The frozen landscape reflected the numbness I lived under, but somehow, the emotional anesthetic provided safety. The changing season would take us further away from Paul. Inexorably, life was moving on without him.

Despite the hope for Paul's eternal future that God's promises had planted in me, I was plagued by thoughts about the futility of the years we spent raising him. All winter, I'd had recurring dreams of giving birth to a baby boy, evidence of my subconscious longing for a do-over.

But if I had it to do all over again, knowing how his life would end, would I do it? Would I choose to carry and give birth to Paul? I can't begin to answer that question. As a finite human being, I'm not capable of weighing and balancing the pros and cons of life's joys and sufferings. I can't determine the value of a life. Though the movie *It's a Wonderful Life* takes a stab at exploring the topic, we can't know what the world would have been like if someone hadn't lived. It is not given to us to make such choices and for that I'm profoundly grateful.

Still, I was tormented by despairing thoughts. What had it all been for? Working around home, I would use a rag to wipe a spill, and remember that cloth was once a diaper for my baby. What did it matter now, that he had caught on to toilet-training in only two days? Finding a 3x5 card covered with math formulas in his tight, bold printing made me wonder why I bothered with the strain of homeschooling him when it left only bitter memories with nothing to show for our efforts.

It was only a short step to allowing suspicion against God to creep into my mind. My heart echoed the psalmist's words in Psalm 89:47b, 48a, "For what futility have You created all the children of men? What man can live and not see death?"

After all, God knew this was coming. He saw us living our lives in hope and expectation, raising our children as though they had a future, training them to be lifelong followers of him. As I continued along this line of reasoning, I could feel my heart shrivel in resentment and distrust. *He had known and I hadn't!* I felt duped. I had been blithely ignorant and unsuspecting of what the future held. I was unaware, as I prayed for Paul and planned his schooling, that all my teaching and training would turn out to be as futile as it now seemed.

But would it have been better if I had known what was to come? Would not the very knowledge of impending disaster be as bad as the actual event? Or worse? Wouldn't I have become an ultra-protective mother, squelching all independence and normal childhood exploration in fear for his safety? And in doing so, wouldn't I have caused all sorts of other kinds of misery in my vain efforts to prevent tragedy? Or perhaps I would have become ultra-permissive, trying desperately to safeguard Paul's good opinion of me by playing the hero. I might have eagerly offered him every privilege and experience in his short life but ended up raising a self-centered brat that nobody could stand.

And I wonder, would I have *wanted* to know what the future held? What if the shroud that obscures our future is, in truth, God's merciful shield?

I wasn't the first to grapple with thoughts of my own finiteness and God's omniscience. I had been echoing John Milton in *Paradise Lost.*

> *"...Let no man seek*
> *Henceforth to be foretold what shall befall*
> *Him or his children – evil, he may be sure,*
> *Which neither his foreknowing can prevent,*
> *And he the future evil shall no less*
> *In apprehension than in substance feel*
> *Grievous to bear..."*

Repeatedly scripture reminded me of God's character. "You are good, and do good." (Psalm 119:68) Gradually, the truth of God's faithfulness overtook my grudge as I remembered his goodness to me over the years. And when I doubted that goodness, I was drawn back to the all-time greatest proof of his love in the sacrificial death of his Son for sinners. No other religious leader and certainly no other god had entered into the misery of this life and then given his life for people who hated him. Yes, I could trust, even blindly, a God who did that for me.

Furthermore, what if, seeing the painful tragic death of my son in the future, he actually wept? Not a hand-wringing, helpless, it's-coming-and-I-can't-do-anything-about-it kind of weeping, but rather, a this-hurts-me-more-than-it-will-hurt-you sort of grief. The kind of weeping that resolves to carry his beloved through sorrow and is determined to use tragedy to bring about triumph. What if he prescribed what to me was a calamity, because it was best for Paul and for me? I had done exactly that years earlier when I put my small son through a surgical procedure for his ultimate good. When Job of ancient times lost all his children and almost all his property, he resolved to trust God in the midst of it. "Though He slay me, yet will I trust Him." (Job 13:15)

Resolving my bitterness over God's keeping me in the dark about the future was one thing. Resolving my own regrets about the past was another. I had been labouring under the belief that Paul's death was directly related to his state of rebellion against us and against God. My every memory of him was stained with blame. With the greening of the grass and trees that spring, my thought patterns began to gain new life too.

Ironically, it began with a large envelope mailed from the coroner's office. "Multiple blunt force injuries," a summary of the eight-page report said. The most significant of these involved the skull, brain and cervical spine. Sickened and dismayed, I read through the long clinical listing, remembering the forensic TV show Paul used to watch. But this was my boy, a real flesh and blood person with a soul! Lacerations, abrasions, broken bones, contusions — very little of his body was unscathed. In later years, I regretted Paul had not signed his driver's license with consent to donate his organs. It would have been a comfort to know some physical part of him still lived and was a blessing to another family.

But the grisly litany in the coroner's report offered one piece of information very important to me. Paul's blood ethanol level was .08, the legal limit for driving, and no illicit substances were detected. We were told this was unlikely to be a drunken state that would have caused serious impairment. It helped to have a tangible hope that Paul had not caused his own death through intoxication.

From that point, I began to look at Paul's life from an angle I hadn't considered before. Where most kids find friendships expanding in high school, his lifelong circle of peers suddenly vanished as his siblings left home. He must have grieved that loss. What if his silence was actually self-control, his way of avoiding lashing out at his parents for the disappointments and frustrations of his life? Could the penchant for punk have been a simple plea for an identity that carried with it a built-in group of friends? In fact, maybe Paul was the one who had been tolerant and patient with me!

One of the sharpest pangs of death is regret. Regret for past words and deeds as well as for things left unsaid and undone.

One Friday evening months before Paul's death, when the air was still and the western sky brooded dark and heavy with a threatening spring storm, I waited in the SUV to take him to youth night at the church. When he opened the passenger door, my heart contracted. He was in full punk array, studded and spiked. I couldn't help but see him as dressed for battle. I refused to take him in that attire. Instead of going indoors to change, he slammed the door and stomped westward toward the sheep pasture. I gave up waiting and went indoors, inwardly tied in tight knots. Did the rumble of thunder cover his swearing into a sky flashing with distant lightning? At last, big, sloppy raindrops forced him, wordless, indoors and to his room. But he never again tried wearing that garb to youth night. Was I squelching his creativity? Majoring on things that were minor? His death put these memories in a different light and filled me with regret. What did it matter how he dressed, I now wondered? Yet while he was alive, we believed we had a responsibility, for the sake of his future, to raise him with a sense of respect and discretion. Hindsight isn't always 20/20.

What was I to do with the regrets roiling within me? With the loss of a young person, there's also lost hope for "the rest of the story." As our other children have matured, we've had conversations with them about what we did wrong as parents. We've had the chance to apologize and be forgiven. They've even told us how things they resented ultimately did them good. But with Paul dead, how could I make it right? Overwhelmed with the pain of the nevermore, one day I asked God to tell Paul I was sorry for being too hard on him, for not recognizing and sympathizing with his losses, for not understanding him and loving him as I ought. My relief was immediate. Peace flooded my soul. I could leave what was unfinished and unresolved with the God who writes last chapters.

With spring, too, came the final step in laying Paul's body to rest. We chose a granite headstone with rough-hewn edges to signify Paul's unfinished life. We ensured the names of his parents and siblings were etched on the back to show he had been cherished by many. And finally, we chose Jude 24 as an epitaph. Not only were we entrusting him to God's care, we were recognizing that God is the only one who can change hard hearts and bring them into right relationship with him.

To Him who is able to keep you…
And to present you faultless
To God our Savior…

When we visited Paul's grave after the stone was placed, I gazed for a long time at the words written in stone, Paul Gabriel Bertin, May 7, 1994 - October 6, 2012.

There was my son's life carved in granite. Just three short, stark lines. The permanent finality of it felt as heavy on me as though I carried the rock on my shoulders.

Chapter 27 – Hungry for Memories

In the movie Philomena, Judy Densch plays a woman who is searching for her son, adopted out as an infant against her will. Eventually she finds him half-way around the world, only to learn he has already died.

There's a scene where Philomena discovers that the journalist who is helping her search, met her son years earlier at a news event. She turns to the writer with urgent longing, almost desperation and asks, "What was he like?"

The journalist protests that all he did was shake hands with him.

As only a mother robbed of a lifetime with her child could plead, Philomena persists. "What was his handshake like?"

So little to go by. Such paltry tidbits to reconstruct a life. My husband and I both felt the pang of grief in that evocative scene. We find ourselves desperately hungry for the least little memory or relic – a handwritten label on a container in the freezer, the story of Paul's funny remarks or a picture of him someone sends us that we've never seen before. Photos of normal teenage fun could sometimes seem eerily prescient; a girl sent us a picture taken on a

Florida beach where the young people with Paul on a summer mission trip were burying someone in the sand. Paul was the entombed one.

Our pastor had been right though. Gradually, many positive memories of Paul were replacing the recent negative ones.

***

Summer 2003 — Between the terrible twos and the turbulent teens, the male of the human species arrives at a place of equanimity. He is capable of self-care and competent at a growing number of tasks that can benefit the family. With, it seems, the exception of one year. Age nine. What is it about a nine-year old boy that makes him go from adorable to annoying in sixty seconds?

It wasn't the heedlessness that was the problem, though Paul's selective hearing, his mother-deafness certainly was frustrating. He could be given a task – even look me in the eye and repeat the instruction – yet carry on doing his own thing, oblivious. Worse than that was his being in his own world. Whatever was motivating that active imagination, it resulted in his getting in everyone's way, running his mouth in droning noise that was frequently punctuated by startlingly explosive sounds. Over time it went beyond irritating to infuriating.

The summer we moved to the country, I noticed increasingly that Paul was getting on the nerves of everyone in the family. Every time I turned around there were outraged groans and remonstrances at him. I'd come to have grave regrets over giving him a motion-activated toy sword he continually brandished. Its loud built-in clanging sound shattered concentration, obliterated conversation and was a shocking nuisance if left lying where unsuspecting folk might brush against it in the night.

But I loved my boy, and I was torn between my own exasperation with him and a motherly protectiveness. I understood our general peevishness toward him, but it saddened me to see that he had become the family pest.

One afternoon when I saw he was safely occupied conquering worlds outdoors, I gathered the rest of us to talk.

"I've seen how annoyed everyone is with Paul and I've been thinking we're just not the best family for him. He needs someone who could appreciate his clever mind and encourage him in his creativity instead of getting irritated with him all the time." I then went on to suggest offering him for adoption to a childless couple we knew who might be more suitable. There was a profound silence. I doubt my husband and the kids thought I was serious, but I hoped such a drastic option might jolt us all into considering our treatment of Paul and our relationship with him.

"He just needs some discipline," one of Paul's brothers, the helpful one, suggested. Not the direction I meant for our meeting to go.

I don't remember anyone falling to their knees in repentance for unloving behavior. We're not a family given to great displays of emotion. But I hoped my melodramatic proposal may have led to a little more patience with him on our part, a little more effort made to include him in our activities. And just maybe, a little more compassion for an active, inventive little boy.

***

Other memories flood my mind in quiet moments alone. It's a winter evening. I picture Paul, about 11, and his brother Jonny, 14, playing on the unheated floor of the kitchen. Jonny can never keep up with Paul's ability when they spend time drawing together, and Paul frequently corrects his older brother's spelling.

"So, I'd challenge him to a game of 'mini-sticks'," Jonny recalls.

This is a game of two-man hockey using short nylon sticks and a ball. Paul keeps a running commentary going while Jonny focuses on his slap-shot. Suddenly the atmosphere turns ugly. Jonny is taunting, laughing, and Paul makes a lunge for him, fury contorting his face. Taller and more agile, Jonny easily eludes him, dashing upstairs. Paul roars in a raging rush after his brother but I stop him, struggling to keep the two apart. I stop the headlong charge, but none of my scolding or appeals to brotherly love can stop the furious fuming.

That level of anger alarmed me. The other boys frequently scuffled over territorial disputes but this seemed different. A murderous, personal wrath. Incidents like this were more than mere spats and they happened too frequently. It seemed like none of our methods of discipline were working.

I feared for his future if his anger was never overcome. What if this were something he never learned to control? How would he function in life, on the job, or in marriage? Was Paul destined to become an abuser or a serial killer? How were we as parents to deal with this?

Helpless and disturbed, I took it to God in prayer. Then one day a couple of years later, I remembered the fury and realized I hadn't seen it in many months. It had simply vanished, replaced with an easy-going camaraderie between brothers and a new ability Paul had found to laugh at himself. Was it merely a matter of growing up, or did the Holy Spirit make that change in him?

***

A couple of neighbours have joined us on a cloudy fall morning in 2006. We're loading hogs to take them for butchering. These are three-hundred-pound animals, their sleek, stream-lined bodies offer no handhold and they're strong. To get them onto the trailer, we devise a ruse. Some of us hold wide pieces of plywood to act as walls, averting the pigs and directing them into a corridor leading toward the transport trailer. Paul, aged twelve, has the job of chasing them down this makeshift hallway. A couple of the hogs refuse to enter and turn back to escape on either side of him. But he's making progress with one pink victim. She's moving along, with Paul a few steps after her. Behind them, the rest of us cleverly maneuver our sheets of plywood to narrow the tunnel.

Suddenly, the sow doubles back, heading straight for Paul. Legs apart, he feints to the left. The pig turns to the right. Paul dodges to the right. The hog heads to the left. Back and forth. She turns around. At last, he thinks she's heading for the trailer. He turns back.

Enough of this, thinks the pig. She wheels and spies the space between Paul's legs.

There's my chance, thinks the pig. She makes for the opening, overestimating its size. For a few brief seconds Paul is weightless, suspended off the earth in an inertia of speed. He feels the rush of air past his ears. His brothers are laughing but he senses the power of the steed beneath him, the smooth and effortless ride through the open field. It lasts only seconds. He flails in vain for a grip on the oval pink flanks. The giant pink pigskin spurts forth from between his legs. With a jolt he lands, his rear in the dirt, stunned.

***

At fifteen, Paul is singularly unenthused at being enrolled in swim lessons for the first time in his life. He is one of the oldest kids in the local home school group and as a swimming beginner, he knows he will be in the lowest level with a bunch of little kids. Swimming just isn't on his radar as a high priority. I talk to him about my own regrets at quitting swimming lessons when I was thirteen for exactly these reasons. Even worse for me, I tell him, my instructor had been a nerdy guy from my class at school. Do I detect one corner of Paul's mouth pull up just slightly? He grudgingly changes his mind and no longer resists enrollment.

I am proud of him for this and I tell him so. Proud of his recognition that learning a skill is more valuable than fear of what people might think of him; proud of his lack of peer dependence; proud of his willingness to cooperate.

When we get to the pool, it turns out they have grouped the classes by age rather than skill level. Paul finds himself in the same class as an old friend, Josh, as well as some cute girls. His skills progress rapidly and he never again complains when I enroll him for subsequent sessions over the next two years.

***

The summer Paul is seventeen, I spend mornings working on math upgrading with him, and afternoons nagging him to mow the grass. It's only the perspective of time that allows me to see that summer as likely the most boring a teen could possibly endure. He doesn't complain, but finds something creative to do with his free time. After watching a movie, he pulls out the family Lego that's been packed away for more than a year now. Drawing from five storage bins, representing nearly thirty years of Lego Christmas gifts (we could have claimed Lego Inc. as a dependent for tax purposes), he recreates the entire battle scene from Shakespeare's Henry IV.

***

One autumn night, perhaps a year before his death, Paul and I are returning from his youth group event on a Friday night. We ride in silence as usual. I mull over the meaning of that silence as I so often do, convinced it is resentment at me that keeps him so tight-lipped. My mind flounders uselessly for a safe topic of conversation; something he won't interpret as nagging or lecturing, but something that might also encourage him somehow.

We turn eastward onto a gravel road in the deepening dusk. Suddenly Paul leans forward and points ahead.

"Look at that," he says, with genuine interest. Intently, I scan the road before us, assuming he's seen a deer or moose. When I raise my eyes, I see what he means. Like a shimmering giant peach floating just above the grasp of bare trees, a full moon hangs, huge and orange against the purpling sky. Entrancing, it is the kind of breath-catching beauty that tightens my throat. I'm pressed to know my smallness, yet at the same time aware of the honour of being given a world of such magnificence. Paul must feel it too. We share awe.

That is to be one of the last memories I have of the two of us sharing anything in harmony. Much later, his brother tells me, "Must have been a Mom-thing. He'd never have said anything like that to me." I treasure the memory even more in the knowledge that it was an intimate moment between mother and son.

***

Months after Paul's funeral, my husband recalled an event that cut through his depression to cheer him. In the spring, shortly after Paul's eighteenth birthday, Mike noticed Paul's electric guitar wasn't working. Together, he helped Paul take it apart and discover a broken wire. He took the time to teach Paul how to solder the wire, feeding the flux onto it under the hot gun. When they plugged the guitar into the amp, Paul played a few chords and his face lit up. He said nothing, but his expression of childish delight was all the thanks Mike needed.

But no amount of memories ever seems to be enough. Worse, as time goes on we find our memories of Paul mistaken or fading.

Six weeks after Paul's funeral, while in Winnipeg for my niece's wedding reception we stayed with my cousin. The funeral earlier that year for her 92-year-old mother, my aunt, had been a landmark occasion of paying tribute to a remarkably godly woman, meeting long-missed relatives, reminiscing and sharing precious memories. I had reveled in the loving bond of family. Now on Marian's dining room buffet, I noticed a small, leather-bound antique photo album. Turning the thick pages of sepia photos of our Russian ancestors, I asked who these people were. Marian didn't know. She could identify only one photo in which her mother was a tiny, blonde girl in a white dress.

Messages from innumerable sympathy cards we had received came to mind. A feeling of futility washed over me with the idea that "we keep our lost loved ones alive in our memory." What is stated in sincerity on some of those cards is an empty promise, given the shortness of life. Please understand that I was touched and truly comforted by the overwhelming love and support we received on the loss of our son. It was especially meaningful when they shared memories of Paul even if bittersweet. But while words are important, they are always inadequate to fully express either depth of loss or depth of love. In the past, I, myself, had often struggled to know what to say or write to the bereaved. Given the utter finality of death, what can possibly be sufficient?

The idea that lost loved ones are kept alive in our memories is well-meant and indeed, memories of Paul are priceless. The fact that we remember for the rest of our lives those who have died is evidence that we as human beings bear an eternal soul. Even more telling is the fact that people of all religious beliefs and none, find themselves speaking to loved ones who have died. We see it in the many Facebook messages written directly to Paul, even years after his death. Instinctively we know the dead go on living, not merely in our fragile memories, but in reality. Yet the idea that "we keep our loved ones alive in our memories" unintentionally does two things. First, it reduces the infinite worth of a human being to mere finite memory. What happens when my memories falter and fade as they're bound to do? Have I then killed my loved one yet again? I'm too frail for such responsibility! Secondly, that sentimental idea diminishes the magnitude of the loss of a precious person, made in God's image. Can memories somehow equal the living, dynamic presence of a person we've known and loved?

Paging through that antique photo album, I pondered the millions and billions of those who are unremembered – peasants and soldiers, nobles of ancient empires and stillborn babies, street children and seniors, unborn babies unnamed and discarded. So many who had lived and died and dreamed and suffered, now forgotten. What was the point of nurturing the memories of our beloved ones, if ultimately, they become merely an unknown photo in a vintage picture album? In a couple of generations, Paul, too, would one day be lost to memory. As I would.

But like finding a mast to cling to in a stormy sea, I grasped hold of the truth that to God, no one is either insignificant in life or forgotten in death. We might feel, "The Lord has forsaken me, and my Lord has forgotten me," but God says, "I will not forget you. See, I have inscribed you on the palms of My hands" (Isaiah 49:16). This gave me a solid hope. My only hope that Paul would never be forgotten. Nor would I.

Paul with his dad
one day old, May 1994

2 years old

The beloved
white blanket

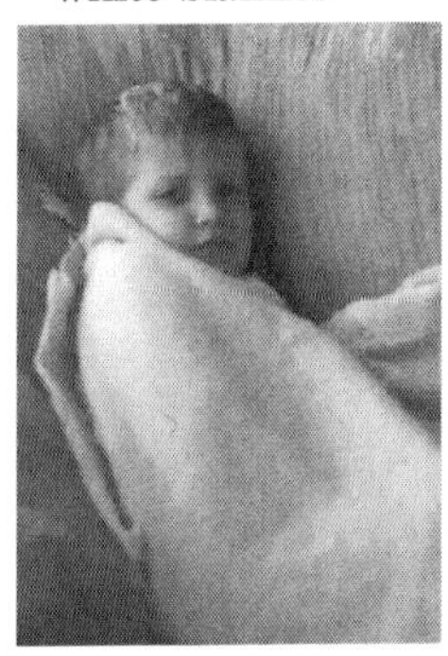

A pirate and his treasures
6 years old

Paul with his 4-H horse, Caspar

One of Paul's maps

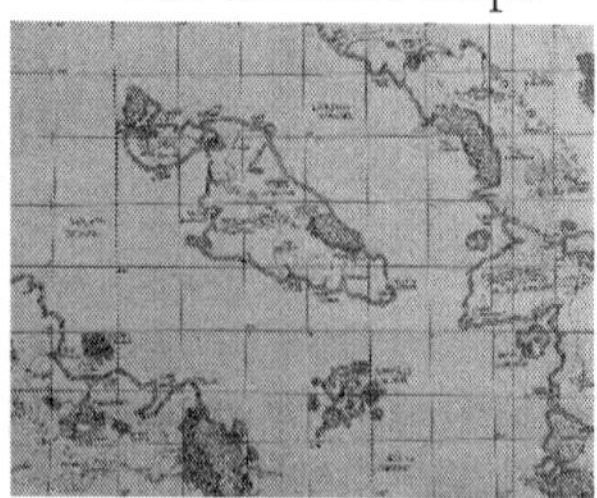

Family 2006: l-r Becky, Tom, Mike, Eleanor, Dan, Jonny
front Paul, Timothy, Ben

Hockey, 2008

Paul and family dog, Ursa

Paul and his siblings, May 2011

Paul with niece Abby, 2011

Diving into local pond, 2011

Experimenting with the punk look, 2012

High school graduation, June 2012

Chapter 28 – Preliminary Hearing

A full year had crawled by without Paul. Late in October 2013, we headed for Provincial Court for the preliminary hearing in the case against the man charged in our son's death. The Crown's office was my first reminder that we were entering another world. One in which violence and vindictiveness were a serious threat. The office was highly secured with bullet-proof glass and a heavy stainless-steel door.

The Crown prosecutor, an earnest, fresh-faced young man, had explained to us that the prelim was simply an opportunity for both the prosecution and the defense to present a summary of their case and allow the judge to decide if there was evidence enough for a trial.

"But," he added, indicating a three-inch thick file folder, "we have a very good case, so there's no danger it'll get thrown out of court." He let slip something else too. It was the first we'd heard that there was evidence the accused had stopped the car and got out to look. The idea that someone had seen Paul lying injured on the road and had callously driven off brought me to tears. I understood then why the nearly empty conference room held two boxes of tissue.

As we were leaving that day, the paralegal showing us out made a comment that lingered in my thoughts.

"Your son didn't do anything wrong. He may have been drinking, but he didn't do anything illegal like driving under the influence." My inclination was to pass this off as irrelevant. Paul had gone against our counsel and while embracing a worldview diametrically opposed to what we'd taught him, he had brought grief and shame on our family. But the more I pondered her words, the more I found solace in them. He hadn't broken the law. There was nothing he could have been charged with.

Later that morning, as we waited in the large, open foyer outside the courtroom, a dark-haired woman sat alone not far from us. Further off, a middle-aged man with a head of thick, white hair, and his wife sat chatting quietly with a pink-cheeked young man. Occasionally they chuckled softly.

After some delay, the prosecutor joined us, explaining he was waiting for one more witness, the person who had been the passenger in the vehicle. By the time we entered the courtroom, this young woman had arrived, slipping past us with her head turned down.

We found seats on the left side of the almost empty court, a room not much bigger than our living room. Its straight, spare furnishings were a stark contrast to the old, ornate courthouse I'd frequented in Winnipeg as a journalism student more than thirty years earlier. That courtroom had seemed to carry the secrets and sins of its participants within the very carving on the walls. Here the bland beige walls had shed the heartaches and fears of those who spent time within, leaving no trace. Back then, too, the cases I'd covered carried no personal meaning for me. Now my heart was to be laid bare.

Another lawyer entered, accompanied by the couple and young man we'd noticed in the foyer. These were the accused and his parents, we realized, when they sat down on the opposite side of the aisle from us. He was not what I was expecting. In a blue, untucked button-front blue shirt and jeans, with clean-cut fair hair, he was not the slovenly, devious ruffian I must have subconsciously pictured. We discovered his parents had flown in from the other side of the country for this brief court appearance. I empathized with them, having to endure the shame of their son's involvement in a crime. Again, I imagined the anguish I would feel if one of our sons had been responsible for someone's death.

The prosecutor opened by presenting the judge with a thick file of notes and information. He briefly explained the events of the early morning of October 6 the year previous, the charges that were laid, and that two witnesses were present in the courtroom that morning.

The judge asked the accused (whom I'll call C.) how he pleaded. Months earlier, in a meeting with the prosecutor, we had learned that at any time before trial, the young man was free to enter a guilty plea. Doing so would spare him and us the stress of going through a trial, save taxpayers' money and court time and could even spell leniency in sentencing for the accused. In fact, in the intervening months, the prosecutor had met with the defense lawyer, telling him we had a very strong case. The defense had urged his client to plead guilty, but, we were told, C.'s father had insisted on the not guilty plea.

When the young man rose to the microphone, he pleaded not guilty and asked to be tried by a judge without jury.

Once the accused has chosen to be tried by a judge without jury, the defense can call for a preliminary hearing if there is doubt that enough evidence exists to convict his client. On seeing two witnesses had shown up, it was clear there was sufficient evidence. The defense lawyer then said his client would waive the right to the full preliminary hearing. It seemed we'd only just sat down when court was adjourned. A court date was set for January 2015. Our hearts sank at the prospect of another fifteen months of waiting and uncertainty.

As we left the courtroom, we passed by the accused. He gave us an almost imperceptible nod that both Mike and I noticed. Was it an acknowledgment of our loss? An expression of sympathy or regret? An apology? Whatever it meant, it kept us kindly disposed toward him.

In the debriefing with the prosecutor later, I seized on his mention of the witness who'd found Paul on the road that night. She was waiting in the next room to meet with the lawyer for the Crown. I asked him if I might have a word with her in private. He hesitated – witnesses and evidence are not to be compromised during a trial - until I explained my purpose. She was my last link with Paul. I felt a strange attachment to this stranger who'd been with my boy as he took his last breaths, whose voice had been the last sound he'd heard on this earth. I desperately wanted to ask her about his final moments.

Our lawyer excused himself and returned saying the woman was willing to meet with us. He cautioned us against discussing anything related to the evidence, however.

Kelly was in her early 40s, dressed in black, heavily made-up and jewelry-bedecked. We sat at a table in the small, bare court anteroom, each somewhat uncertain.

"I am so glad to meet you," I began.

"I'm so sorry!" she said, with feeling.

Kelly's kind sympathy put me at greater ease. I told her I'd been wondering so many things about that night.

"I was coming home from work," she said, "when I saw something up ahead on the bridge. I was nervous because I'd heard how people set up a scenario to gain sympathy so women stop to help and then they assault them. But as I got closer, I could see it was real. So, I parked my car across the lane your son was in and called 911."

I was hungry for something, anything to comfort me and add to my meager trove of Paul memories. "Did he – did he say anything?" I asked. I still hoped for some clue, some indication that Paul had had some conscious moments, or even unconscious, but spiritually aware moments.

"No, he didn't," she said. Then she added a curious thing. "But he looked so peaceful. He looked like an angel."

This was what she'd told our sons when she visited them the year before. I thought it was significant that the story hadn't changed. Clearly, something had made an impression on this woman. But I couldn't really picture what she was describing. What did "looked like an angel" mean?

She gazed directly into my eyes. "He changed my life, you know."

Her words grabbed my attention. Since the day we heard Paul had been killed, I had prayed something good would come out of his life and death. Yet in the year since then, I had seen no change in the things I had in mind. So just a few days before the preliminary hearing, I had asked God to *show* me some way in which Paul's life had made a difference.

She pulled out her phone. "I have a picture of him on my phone. Do you want to see it?"

She took a picture of him as he lay on a street, the life ebbing out of him? What kind of a macabre thing to do was that? Yet it must have meant that his body, his life made an enormous impact on her. Particularly the fact that she'd kept it on her phone for over a year.

But do I want to see him, mutilated, in pain, dying?

Suspended in the shock and uncertainty of the possibility, I couldn't answer, but my hesitation didn't seem to bother Kelly. She set aside her phone and I never did see the photo. Then she went on to explain the way Paul had changed her life. She told us she had three school-age children, the oldest a young teen.

"I quit my job as a bartender and took a day job so I could spend more time with my kids."

I knew that simple statement covered a great depth of struggle and sacrifice. Working the night shift in a bar is highly lucrative in tips. To let go of that for daytime work would almost certainly mean a considerable cut in salary but she was willing to exchange money for the sake of precious time with her children. It was obvious to me this change represented a tremendous paradigm shift for her.

Moved, I reached across the small table to grasp her arm.

"I've been praying that something good would come of this. Thank you so much for telling me that." We rose, two mothers bound together by a common desire to shield and love our children, and hugged each other tightly.

Chapter 29 – Comfort from the Word

Although we had a large family, a daughter and six sons, we didn't have any to spare. Each is unique, irreplaceable. Paul's absence left a giant hole in our family, a wound that would show itself still jagged and raw at his brother's wedding the summer of 2014. I had always been rather proud of my collection of fine lads. But there was a poignancy in the line-up of handsome groom and five groomsmen. This time it included a friend in the place where Paul should have been.

Gradually, the fog of early grief had faded away to be replaced with frequent stark reminders of the new reality we lived in. It seems the human psyche can get used to anything. And I did, in a sense, get used to having one son gone. But somehow the pain of grief intensified. I was less disturbed about Paul's eternal state after the assurance about God's trustworthy goodness that I'd received from the book of Hosea. My initial numbness had kept me from thinking about the facts of his death but now these and other sorrows rushed at me in unguarded moments. Overheard words would assail me with darts of grief: Tears sprang to my eyes one day as I listened to a pregnant mom tell her small child that the new baby would "be with us forever." I, too, once made that assumption. Such an innocent explanation, yet it tore at my insides. I quickly turned away so the tears in my eyes wouldn't betray me and destroy the young woman's joy and trust in the future.

In many ways, God kept soothing these grief pangs with his love and truth. Sometimes it was through the kindness of fellow believers months after the funeral, a meal brought, a pot of spring flowers, a phone-call or message that we were being prayed for and weren't forgotten. Most often however, comfort came through God's written word. Still, not all my questions were answered and sometimes scripture raised new struggles.

My journal entry from May 29, 2014 reveals one such wrestling match.

Psalm 72:12-14

For He will deliver the needy when he cries

But you didn't, Lord! When that car first struck him and he was thrown up against its windshield, there must have been a terrible cry. Did you hear it? And what does this mean about deliverance? My boy wasn't delivered! I continue reading.

The poor also, and him who has no helper.

Paul had no one to help him there all alone, battered and bleeding on that chilly night.

He will spare the poor and needy.

But Lord, it doesn't seem to me that you spared him!

And will save the souls of the needy.

Okay, I begin to see, Lord. Paul certainly was needy, both physically and spiritually. Aren't we all desperately needy for God to save our souls? Did you make him aware of his need?

He will redeem their life from oppression and violence.

Ah, here we have it – the acknowledgment that oppression and violence are a reality in this world. Not everybody is spared suffering. The promise is that you will redeem ("buy back," "make good out of") whatever sin and suffering does to your people. Paul certainly experienced violence, but is this your promise to bring good out of it?

And precious shall be their blood in His sight

Blood was shed! Precious. Paul's blood was precious to you – of great value or worth. You saw his life-blood flowing out of him there on the road — were you moved with compassion? Precious means beloved, much prized. There's emotion there. Did you weep that night, Lord? "In His sight" means you saw it all, you were there with him. You didn't miss a thing. Thank you, Lord Jesus, for loving him and being there with him when no one else could!

As I meditated on the psalm, the words "will save" seemed definite and decisive to me. Since it's an obvious fact that no one is spared all physical suffering, clearly this meant spiritual salvation. Did God save Paul in those final moments? Or perhaps God had already done so years earlier? Oh, how I wanted to believe that! I knew God was powerful enough to overcome a rebel's resistance and that a person's salvation comes about because of God's work within them. I believed it could even be accomplished while a person was unconscious.

But my desire for certainty kept colliding with the closed-to-me door of the inscrutable will of God. "The secret things belong to the Lord our God, but those things which are revealed belong to us and to our children forever" (Deuteronomy 29:29). Again and again, I had to be reminded that not only does he do as he pleases (Psalm 115:3) but he is wholly good (Psalm 119:68). I clung to the bedrock certainty of his trustworthy character.

Chapter 30 – Before the Judge

Everyday life is casual and humdrum. It runs swiftly without much reflection, fanfare or formality. And if Facebook posts and Hollywood movies are the standard, it's got to be funny. How rare it is, in the course of everyday life, to catch even a fleeting glimpse of ceremony, reverence, gravitas.

Opening day of the January 13, 2015 trial of the young man charged in the death of our son offered us that glimpse.

In provincial court, we stand when the judge enters the courtroom. We sit only when he sits. If we must leave while court is in session we turn and bow to him before we do so. All evidence is offered to him and everything that takes place is by his permission.

All this ceremony reminded me of what we'd discussed in the women's Bible study I had led just the day before.

"I watched till thrones were put in place, and the Ancient of Days was seated; His garment was white as snow, And the hair of His head was like pure wool. His throne was a fiery flame, its wheels a burning fire; A fiery stream issued and came forth from before

Him; Ten thousand times ten thousand stood before Him. The court was seated and the books were opened." (Daniel 7)

Someday each one of us will stand before the Ultimate Judge, as the accused stood before this Court of Queen's Bench justice. In that day, perfect justice will reign because we will be in the presence of a Judge who knows all things, including our very thoughts and intentions, past, present and future.

For this day, we were in an earthly courtroom which, as formal as it was, came nowhere close to that fearsome preview of a final judgment day. Here, the lawyers wore long black robes and under them, white wing-tip collars, short black jackets with slits under the arms that showed the white of their shirts, and dark trousers. Witnesses were asked, "Will you swear on the Bible?" All of them did, revealing a heartening respect for God's Word. I wondered what other option there would have been to secure a person's sincerity? What else could possibly undergird and symbolize our entire system of law and government?

Although our three sons and their wives who lived locally were unable to attend court due to work commitments, I was touched and encouraged by the presence of neighbours and friends who came to support us. At an earlier meeting, the prosecutor had mentioned to us that the presence of family and friends in court was a way to make a statement that the victim mattered. It could even affect sentencing

The Crown's case against C. involved two charges. He was accused of public mischief for falsely reporting his car stolen to divert suspicion away from himself, which carried a maximum penalty of five years in prison. Secondly, he was charged with failure to give assistance whereby he intended to escape civil or criminal liability by failing to stop the vehicle, give his name and address and offer assistance. The defense did not contest the public mischief charge relating to that false report, in effect pleading guilty to it. Later, we were told the defense attorney was very gentlemanly; not talking down to witnesses as so many do. This spared us the stress of an antagonistic trial for which we were grateful.

The first witness called was the bartender who first found Paul on the road as she was coming home from work that early morning of October 6, 2012. Seated directly behind the prosecutor, I caught a glimpse of the photo he picked up to have her identify the body. My stomach lurched. There was far more blood than I'd been led to believe. She gave her answers clearly and firmly. Paul had been lying in the middle of the left-hand driving lane, parallel to the lane. This piece of information troubled me. It confirmed my fear that Paul was not where he should have been – on a sidewalk, or at least on the narrower, emergency lane on the right side of the bridge. It brought back the fear that the defense could make a case for Paul's having been too drunk to know what he was doing, making him ultimately responsible for his own death.

The Crown's second witness was a young woman who had been a passenger in the vehicle that struck Paul. Prior to the trial, we had seen her wiping tears away as we waited for the courtroom to open. She fidgeted as she testified that she had been very intoxicated that night. She'd had eight to nine beers at a friend's, she said, before going to the downtown club where she drank more and met the accused through an on-line dating app.

"I used to drink quite heavily," she said.

During a morning recess when we were meeting with the prosecutor, we were touched when this young lady came into the anteroom to tearfully whisper to us, "I'm so sorry." Parents often warn young girls of risky behaviours that could end in date rape or car wreck but who could anticipate such a lifelong sorrow — being in a vehicle that kills someone? I hoped her statement "I *used* to drink quite heavily" meant it was a thing of the past and that in this, too, Paul's life and death may have played a positive role.

When she heard the "thud" of collision, she continued, she'd had her head down, texting, so she didn't see what had been struck. She said the accused had stopped the car, gotten out to look and returned, telling her he thought he'd hit an animal.

As he listened to the testimonies once court resumed after a recess, the accused appeared casual, leaning back in his black padded office chair. But he chewed his fingernails almost constantly. I couldn't blame him. How shameful it must have been for him to listen to this very public exposure of one damning lie after another when his intent must surely have been to cover his crime. And I thought of the times in my own life when I'd lied to hide my sin. He must have been relieved his parents were not in the court room to hear it all. It was curious to us that they sat in the foyer throughout the court proceedings. Later, the prosecutor told us the accused's lawyer had requested the parents not be present in the courtroom. He suspected it was due to the father being a "high maintenance" individual who might have become disruptive. It certainly spared them the disgrace of hearing their son's lies.

In public court, C. now had to listen to his own incriminating words. A 911 call from later in the day of the crime recorded the accused reporting in detail the "theft" of his car. At great length, he speculated on the possible ways a thief might have found the spare key in a magnetic key box located beneath his car.

The collision analysis expert gave graphic descriptions of how our son was hit. Since Paul's death, the stomach-clenching I'd experienced whenever I drove near the Taylor Street Bridge in Red Deer had caused me to avoid it. If mention of "the body", "the deceased" or "the victim"" tightened my insides, how much more the gruesome scene so accurately reconstructed. But the police expert added a new piece of information. In his opinion, our boy was hit twice, the second time just driven over by another vehicle, scraping his chest and arm. That was agonizing to hear. Someone else had driven over my dying boy, perhaps not even noticing there was anything on the road!

Paul's shoes had been found some distance away from his body. How hard must a body be struck for their shoes to go flying, I wondered in horror. We learned, however, that ejection of shoes is a common occurrence on impact. The collision analyst testified that a "fairly large mass of green hair was stuck in the windshield" of the car when it was later found. Oh, that green hair! I couldn't have known that the hated green would be an important clue in later finding the car that killed my son.

The first day of court was over. We went home exhausted and apprehensive at the prospect of tomorrow's Medical Examiner's testimony.

I clung to the ancient words of comfort in my weakness. "My flesh and my heart fail; but God is the strength of my heart and my portion forever." (Psalm 73:26)

Chapter 31 – A Web of Lies

The second morning of court, January 14, we had lost the nervousness that comes of everything being unfamiliar. But we were dreading the Medical Examiner's report, knowing it would detail and explain Paul's injuries. Yet that wasn't first on the agenda. And it wasn't the worst.

Court opened with an audio interview conducted in an RCMP officer's car between a cop and the accused on Saturday, Oct. 6, 2012. The officer, who was working on his scheduled day off because of this investigation, explained most kindly and respectfully to the accused that the car he had reported stolen had been located.

"Cool," said the young man.

There was something so pitiful about hearing someone make such bold-faced lies when the police officer in the interview, and everyone later in court, knew none of it was true. Trying to cover sin with lies had backfired, making the crime even more despicable.

The officer urged C. to be sure to tell the truth, that he (the cop) was a straight-shooter who would only tell the truth and expected the same. The accused was quite agreeable to all this, stating that he had and would tell only the truth.

Then the cop gave him the bad news.

"Your vehicle was involved in a criminal offense," the officer said.

"Was it wrecked?" C. asked, with expressions of shock. "I don't wanna get involved in anything like that. I just wanna get my car back."

"Well, you *are* involved," the cop said, "because your car was used in a criminal activity."

"Well, I come from New Brunswick," C. said, "and had some trouble with the law there. I came here to start a new life, so I don't want to get involved in anything to do with court."

This was unutterably sad to me. I completely understand the desire to get away somewhere for a fresh start. We'd done something similar when we moved to the country in 2003 in an effort to keep our children from negative influences. The problem is, we take ourselves with us. Only a change of heart spawns a new life.

The cop repeated several times to this young man that he now *was* involved. The officer urged C., while still telling him it was his choice, to come to the police station and make a statement. The accused kept repeating his not wanting to get involved.

The officer, infinitely patient and reasonable, praised C. as a "decent kind of guy," to which the accused eagerly agreed. But even that didn't elicit any admission of guilt. The cop asked C. if he would be willing to come in for a "truth verifier," explaining that's what they call a polygraph, rather than a lie detector. More demurring on the part of the accused.

Leaving his card with C., the cop left, suggesting that C. might think of something else and could contact police.

By Sunday, October 7, C. had called his parents in New Brunswick who had hooked him up with a lawyer, so he phoned the officer back and was willing to come to the station to make a statement.

The video interview opens with a view from above.

C. is alone at a table in a bare room wearing a black T-shirt. He is wiping his eyes and snuffling a bit.

The cop, in civilian clothes, enters and takes a seat nearby. "I'm really glad you came in. You've manned up and that's really good. I have to tell you the investigation keeps on going." (I was so impressed with the patience and caution the police showed throughout this case. It couldn't have been easy to listen to lies and evasion, yet they showed restraint and did not lose patience or exhibit frustration which could have jeopardized the case.)

Now the officer asks C. to tell his story of the events of October 5th and 6th. This time there's a difference.

The accused says he was at the Lotus Club, drinking, met a girl on an on-line dating app, didn't know her name or really much of what she looked like. *People do this? Hop into cars with strangers who have been drinking?* This seemed to me as risky for guys as it is for girls.

They got in his car to go up to a buddy's for an after party since bars were closing at two a.m. On Taylor Bridge, a "dark figure" very suddenly appeared.

C. emphasizes that he has his Class 1 license and always keeps his eyes on the road, never speeding. When the dark figure appeared, he hit it, but thought it was an animal. He relates that the girl, in fact, said, "what the h— was that? It must have been an animal."

He says he knew it was no small animal like a dog or cat or porcupine and thought it must have been a deer or "a black bear, standing up."

He kept driving, he says, got to his buddy's, sent the girl home (in a cab, she had testified) and parked his car, then walked to his own home.

After questioning this account on various points, the cop eventually informs him that, "Someone is no longer alive."

At this point, my stomach was swirling. That someone was my boy! And I was only too keenly aware that he was no longer alive. Hearing those raw words pierced my heart yet again.

With those words, C. begins sobbing, wiping tears. The officer pats him on the shoulder, kindly asking him if he's okay. C asks for a garbage can to put his used tissue in.

Again, C. insists he thought it was an animal.

The officer gently says, "I'm placing you under arrest." This is nothing like cop shows on TV. After reading him his rights, and C. agreeing he wants to talk to a lawyer, the cop asks, "Is there anything you want to tell the family of the deceased?"

This was when I leaned forward to hear how he might answer. It could have been the time for a confession, an admission of guilt, an apology.

"They probably hate me and want me dead!" he sobs.

I shook my head "no" at this. We didn't hate him, or want yet another person dead. But, as my husband later pointed out, the accused was still entirely focused on himself. At the time that interview took place, we were reeling in shock and devastation at the loss of our son and brother. Hating the driver and wanting him dead was the last thing on our minds.

"You can't fix it," he continues. "I don't even know what to say."

Well, at least on that point we had something in common! Not being able to fix it is something I learned as a six-year-old. Running across the farmyard where I grew up, a brood of pet Bantam chicks scampered along beside me when I accidentally stepped on one. In disbelief, I agonized over the fluffy little creature. One moment it was bouncing along beside me full of energy, the next minute it was still and lifeless at my feet. How could it be? What could be done? I desperately longed to reverse time just a few moments so I could undo my deed. But there was no going back. Since October 2012, death's sheer irrevocability was something we too had been trying to grasp. How very far-reaching are the actions of a moment!

At a later point in the interview, C. asks how old the person was. When the cop tells him he was eighteen, there are serious tears. (Earlier, the passenger witness had referred to the fact that after the collision, the accused had got out of his car and looked. Knowing he had seen Paul immediately after impact, I thought these tears may have been a genuine expression of horror and grief that such a young person had died.)

The last witness in court that day, the one we had most dreaded, was the Calgary Medical Examiner, via Skype. She testified that Paul was killed by severe skull and brain injury and a broken neck. There were many other injuries, and she confirmed what we had heard the day previous. Describing face and chest abrasion, she said Paul was probably driven over by another vehicle. These injuries ran parallel to the body, so no tires went over him.

It was excruciating to hear that someone else had cavalierly driven over our boy, either glibly unaware, or aware there was a body but deliberately avoiding involvement, perhaps because of their own drunken state. Somewhere, that driver is still out there, never to be held accountable for what they did. Did the person read about the incident in the newspaper and come to a horrible realization? Does he or she still have nightmares about it or do they simply rationalize it away?

That afternoon, following the evidence presented by the prosecution, the defense was supposed to offer evidence. There was none to offer. Court was adjourned until the next day.

What could a mom say to these things? My heart felt as exposed and bleeding as my boy had been lying on that bridge. And yet, in all of it, I clung to God's promise, as true for me as it had been for Paul that dark morning.

> *Even though I walk through the valley of the shadow of death, I will fear no evil;*
> *For You are with me…" (Psalm 23:4)*

Chapter 32 – On the Run

I don't want to go, I told my husband when he got up early that third morning, January 15, and got ready for court.

But go we did. The raw emotion of the ordeal was like having your insides pulled outside your body and stroked with a wire brush. I'd had more than enough of it that week.

We arrived to find a very crowded Provincial courthouse. They were selecting a jury for a local bombing murder case. Someone had sent a bomb in a package to a young wheelchair-bound woman, killing her in to get her life insurance. It's a foreign world in that place. And perhaps the theme of that day in court was the awareness that there are people who live, raise their children and generally operate on an entirely different value system than we do.

We were happy to have one of our younger sons join us that day in the courtroom. It felt so good to have one of our *living* sons with us.

But I'd barely had a chance to greet him when the Crown attorney gave us news that had surprised even him. It was five minutes past starting time and he'd just discovered the accused was not present. The prosecutor said although he'd anticipated this happening in some of his other cases, he'd never seen it happen in all his years of practice and he had not expected it in this case.

When the judge entered there was some discussion between him and the two lawyers about what to do. We recessed for another half hour, with the judge hoping it was simply January road conditions or some other unforeseen event making him late. For us, the roads on the hour-long drive into town had been bare and dry. I was impressed with the judge's generous attitude.

But no. The accused never showed up.

Everyone was taken by surprise, even the defense lawyer. Apparently, C.'s parents had arrived at court earlier, but left again, as they were scheduled to fly home that day. They knew as little about his whereabouts as everyone else. They did say their son had been very stressed and hadn't been sleeping well. I could only imagine. Neither had we.

When we first came to court, we had held in our hearts a willingness to forgive. I was all too aware of my own sin and the many foolish things I had done when I was younger or that my husband or children had done, that so easily could have ended tragically. And even though the sins we all daily commit may not be criminal offenses, who among us is entirely guiltless? So, conscious of all I'd been forgiven of, I put myself in the shoes of the accused and his parents. I imagined the heartache they must have been experiencing at the thought of their son being responsible for someone's death. No doubt they would feel shame and anguish at the prospect of prison time for him, but also, fear of the very real possibility of abuse and mistreatment in such a dreaded place.

Yet the day before, something had occurred to make me aware that other parents might not hold that same perspective. As I trudged up the long, wide flight of stairs to the second-floor courtroom after a recess, I was met by the piercing gaze of the accused's father, seated in the waiting area on the second floor. His unrelenting black eyes seemed to bore into me. I became uncomfortable and looked away. It was the first time I considered the possibility they could be angry at our son and at us. Were they outraged that their son's life was now being messed up simply because of a careless pedestrian out on the road late at night? Were they right? These thoughts threatened my resolve to have a forgiving heart. I had to remind myself that I, too, had been a sinner in need of mercy. In fact, while I was still a sinner and an enemy of God, Christ gave his life for me. I was under obligation to forgive.

Finally, that day a warrant was issued for C.'s arrest. We had no idea when or if they would find him. By way of providing ourselves hope and a reprieve from the heaviness of court, we had scheduled our vacation to see our grandchildren in Texas for the day after the trial was to close. Now we had to leave this unsettled matter behind. Throughout our travel time, I thought about the freedom a clear conscience allows. In contrast, fleeing police would mean a restless watchfulness, trying to devise ways of evading the law.

Naturally, it was only a matter of time. Two weeks later, the accused was apprehended in Red Deer. He would have to sit in jail nearly three months until the new date in April, set for closing arguments and a verdict to complete this trial. And of course, he might face new charges for absconding from court that day. My heart grieved for such a fearful, confused and selfish young man.

What he'd done that day only reinforced the pattern of behaviour he was charged with: running away and covering his crimes. It would most likely affect the judge's sentencing.

Obviously, the actions of the accused couldn't be blamed entirely on his parents. He was legally an adult. But he had demonstrated a pattern of running from responsibility for his actions. It reinforced for me the belief that parents do a great disservice to their children if they protect them from the consequences of their actions. A beam of encouragement cut through years of self-recrimination about our parenting. Had we been too hard on our children, I often wondered. Had we prohibited too much? Now I thought perhaps our emphasis on attending to the development of our kids' character hadn't been far wrong. We had taken seriously the Bible's admonitions to discipline our children.

> *"My son, do not despise the chastening of the Lord, nor detest His correction; For whom the Lord loves He corrects, just as a father the son in whom he delights." (Proverbs 3:11, 12)*

Chapter 33 – Slow Wheels of Justice

The court case against the one accused in the death of our son was set to resume April 2, 2015. Because of the backlog of court cases, it didn't. June 5 was set as the next court date. C.'s refusal to show up for court three months earlier meant neither the prosecutor nor the judge felt any urgency to speed the process along. The young man languished in the Provincial Remand Center in Red Deer, a facility known for its overcrowding. Inmates have no opportunity to go outdoors and no programs or activities are provided.

The roster just outside the courtroom had carried the listing, C. vs. the Crown, making it appear this case was between the court and the accused alone. Perhaps I wasn't the only one to experience an odd sense of exclusion at seeing that. It may have been part of the motivation, years earlier, to address victim impact. There is a strange bond between the perpetrator and victim in a crime. It's not voluntary or pleasant, but it is there. What was happening in this case intimately affected us. We no longer had Paul to talk to, to be involved with. As poor a substitute as it was, following the court case regarding his death was the closest we could come to having a tangible, ongoing relationship with our son. So, when we came and went from a court date that turned out to be a non-event and the case was postponed yet again, we were troubled. Not that we expected the outcome of the case to provide "satisfaction," just settlement. And with the postponement, it was still unfinished business.

I am, however, grateful we live in a country where a person is innocent until proven guilty. We truly wanted justice for the accused as well as our son. But there had been off-the-record comments from those involved in the justice system that continued to taint our view of the young man. The likelihood that he had been quite drunk was impossible to prove because of his having run from the scene. In a sense, the accused was rewarded for having fled. We were also told there were texts (while driving) on his phone, inadmissible in court, indicating he had been on his way to an afterparty where drugs were promised. It seemed unfair that these facts could not come to light.

Still, I was thoroughly impressed with the police investigation, their keeping in contact with us, the prosecution's scrupulous attention to detail and, court date postponements notwithstanding, the whole justice system in general. I'm aware that this is not the perspective we hear much about, but it was our experience. I suspect when someone has been a victim of a crime, they feel like lashing out at whoever crosses their path and since they have no access to the perpetrator, those in the justice system receive the brunt of their anger.

While we waited, life went on. We enjoyed vivid days with our children and grandchildren, full of lively fun and the quaint sayings of preschoolers, a welcome reprieve from the court's focus on death and crime. We worked on our house, pursued hobbies, served in our church. I finished a novel that had provided blessed escape from the heaviness of grief, and began pitching it to agents. I also became more established in my new job at our local library. But we began to realize there was, and always would be an undercurrent of sorrow in our lives. Early on, someone had said, "you never get over it." At the time I found the comment cruel. It snatched my hope of "recovery" and flung it into a sea of hopelessness.

But I began to remember my grandparents in a new light. There had always been wisps of mystery surrounding their oldest daughter, Annie, just two years younger than my father. Not mystery in the cause of death; she had died of a sudden and very brief illness at the age of twenty-one. Rather, it was a hush that muffled her name and memory. She was simply not spoken of, though the black-and-white portrait of her pure-skinned young face framed by softly curled hair was kept in view in Oma and Opa's living room. Now I wondered how it was for my grandparents as the years went on when the family gathered at holidays. Most certainly, they could never forget their girl as we would never forget our son. With a new empathy I could now guess their feelings as they watched their married sons and later their daughter, have children and move on in life. I felt privy to the strange mixture of pleasure and pain they would have known, enjoying their expanding family, yet wondering who Annie might have married, what children she might have had. Perhaps there would have been a cousin my age after all.

Today we make much of the need to talk about our feelings. And I certainly have valued the burden-sharing such talk has allowed me. Yet I can't object to my grandparents' careful guarding of their grief. There is a sense in which such a loss is impossible to speak of. How can words express the slicing of the heart? Contrarily, at the same time, we longed for people to allow us to talk about Paul even at the risk of our tears. We dreaded his being forgotten and life closing over the spot where he had been as though he'd never lived. One of the best responses I received was from a stranger who had asked about my children.

"What was Paul good at?" she asked me. The question took me off guard. I had been accustomed to thinking of and explaining the regrets I'd had about his life. But she'd cracked open the rusty treasure box of my pride in him. I mentioned his drawing ability and his musical talent. Her question twigged the memory of his spot-on mimicry – he used to inject "Toodle-pip!" or some such humorous movie quip into daily life with just the right accent and tone. It was an unexpected pleasure to have an opportunity to tell someone about him and a joy to recount some of his positive characteristics.

And so, we continued to wait for the slow wheels of justice. "But as for me, I trust in You, O Lord; I say, 'You are my God.' My times are in Your hand." Psalm 31:14, 15

Chapter 34 – A Surprise Move

Just before court was to convene June 5, the Crown prosecutor asked us to meet with him. Something had come up two weeks prior through a private investigator and he didn't want the possible appearance of it in court to disturb us.

But my stomach constricted thinking of the possibilities of what this "new evidence" might be. How might it affect the case at this late stage? And who hired a PI? It was not the prosecution who hired one; their case had been solid from the outset. We could only guess who might have been scrambling to find some sort of exonerating information.

Coincidentally, the prosecutor explained, C. was in detention with the current boyfriend of Paul's former girlfriend, the one who had broken up with Paul a few weeks before he died. In conversation with C., this boyfriend claimed to know something about the case and offered a note to the PI.

Unsigned, the note was about six lines on crumpled paper saying the writer couldn't go on "without her" because life would be "meaningless." Early in their investigation, the police had already questioned our sons about the possibility of Paul having committed suicide. The boys had recoiled at such an idea. By all accounts, Paul had been happy and excited that day, October 5, 2012. He'd just bought a new guitar amp and for the first time that night, his band had played a song he himself had written.

At first it was an alarming idea that this could be used as evidence. Of what? We had no idea. But once we saw the note, there was no worry. It seemed a simple matter to prove it was not Paul's handwriting. His was a rather cramped, angular all-caps printing while this was a wide-spaced, rounded, upper- and lower-case printing. I thought there was something vaguely familiar about this writing. Where had I seen it before? Besides the marked difference in hand-writing, there were at least two spelling errors in the note. This was a dead giveaway that Paul had not penned it. At six years old, Paul could spell xenophobic and knew what it meant. He didn't make spelling mistakes.

What was mystifying to us was the motive of the person who produced the note. How could it possibly benefit the fellow inmate? When we asked how this might be used in the case, the prosecutor suggested the defense might try to show Paul's death was going to happen inevitably; that he was a suicide looking for a place to happen. The very suggestion of suicide evoked new heartache. Although Paul's brothers had been certain of his good-humour, I wondered if it might be true. Had he carried an underlying guilt for his rejection of all he'd been raised to believe? The possibility lent an edge of nervous uncertainty to court proceedings that day.

When court opened, a sheriff brought in the accused wearing a dark sweater, his leg shackles rattling as he took his place in the glass-walled prisoner's dock. He scanned the courtroom and smiled at his mother. Perhaps he hadn't seen his parents in the nine months since the opening of the case in January.

The Crown's main argument that morning centered on the accused *knowing* he'd struck a person and that he was willfully blind to that truth.

"Mr. C. is a liar," the prosecutor said. What a damning summation of character to hear publicly stated. But I guess that's what we call someone who lies. C.'s post-offense conduct of lying to police and trying to cover up his crime by claiming his vehicle stolen showed he was trying to escape criminal justice, the prosecutor concluded.

I had been nervous about the defense attorney's argument. Would he try to lay the blame on Paul in some way?

When the lawyer for the defense rose to address the court, he emphasized that drivers do not expect pedestrians to be about at two a.m. and that the bridge not only had no sidewalks on the northbound side, but in addition, carried a sign saying Do Not Walk. The defense primarily argued that C. thought he'd hit an animal and then panicked. C's lawyer did not try to explain why hitting an animal would induce panic. But hearing him cast doubt on the prosecution's evidence, especially that given by a witness who, by her own admission had been quite intoxicated at the time of the collision, did raise doubts in my mind. Would the case be thrown out due to an unreliable witness? While the defense explained C.'s actions as stemming from panic and confusion, I remembered my own thoughts when the police had arrived at our door that October morning, before I understood what it was they were trying to tell us. I had thought one of our sons had hit someone, panicked and run away. Not that it would have made it a right thing to do, only that it would have been understandable.

As it turned out, there was never any mention of the suicide note in court at all. I was grateful we were not left with the heartache and guilt feelings that follow the family of one who takes his own life.

When the judge returned from deliberation that afternoon, he carefully went through the evidence point by point. Just as the prosecutor had presented, the judge stated that the accused *intended* to mislead police in order to deflect attention from himself and the more serious criminal offense.

He went on to say the accused "has shown himself to be a liar." Claiming he thought he'd hit an animal was "totally lacking in credibility."

"I don't believe his claim that he didn't stop," the judge continued. "I don't accept that he might not have seen the body." Every mention of the deceased, or the body, throughout this recap of the evidence, was once again a piercing reminder that this was our boy they were talking about. By this time, we were in tears, my husband especially.

Then without fanfare or slamming of the gavel, C. was found guilty on both charges; public mischief as well as failure to give assistance. Sentencing would take place on July 22.

As we anticipated, there was no joy in the prospect of a young man going to prison. There was, though, a sense that it is fitting and right that someone should be held accountable for actions involving a person's death.

As it stood, C was not being held responsible for the death of our son. Running from the scene precluded that charge. If the relatively new statute of "failure to give assistance" had not been in place, there would have been only the public mischief charge with a penalty of perhaps six months.

Because of C's fleeing the scene and the web of lies that followed, we, Paul's family, have paid certain consequences beyond the permanent loss of our son, brother, grandson, nephew, uncle. We were now plagued by the new image of our boy lying on a street, hurt and cold and alone. Adding to our grief was finding out in the trial that another vehicle drove over him, a direct result of the accused having left the scene. Only the accused could have told us which part of the road Paul was walking on that night. And we will never know whether Paul was briefly conscious, or whether he said any last words, something I desperately longed to know.

Amid all the sorrow and suffering, it was infinitely comforting to be reminded that my heavenly Father understood my pain. He watched his precious, innocent son suffer and die at the cruel hands of mankind. While we waited, I resolved to be content to leave justice in the hands of imperfect human institutions, knowing that ultimate justice awaits the return of "…the Lord Jesus Christ, who will judge the living and the dead." (2 Timothy 4:1)

Chapter 35 – Adding Insult to Injury

A day prior to the July 22 court date, Mike received another call from the Crown prosecutor. We needn't show up for court the next day, he informed us. All that would happen would be that C. would officially fire his lawyer. He had a new one lined up who would offer new "evidence" in the case.

We thought we could guess the direction this would go. Yet all the evidence had already been presented in January, and a verdict had been reached. Did he now plan to use that "suicide note" to prove Paul was suicidal? That it was inevitable he would fling himself in front of a car and C. was just the unlucky motorist who had done the deed? The possibility of his using that line of argument to further wiggle out of responsibility was deeply hurtful. For nearly three years we had been grieving the loss of our boy. To intimate that he had wanted to die was to load us with a new dimension of grief and turmoil that suicide always leaves in its wake— guilt. I know God can give comfort and hope even in those cases, but I recoiled from added struggles. We felt sure the note would easily be proven a fake, but it introduced doubts and it was a stress we didn't need.

Not only that, but we had been involved with the justice system for three years already, what with no-shows and delays. Although a guilty verdict and sentencing would not change our lives in any way, there was that odd sense of being bound to this young man by his involvement in Paul's death. It seemed we were in a suspended state of unfinished business, waiting for the case to be finally settled.

And the scheme made no sense. The case never had been about the collision that killed our son. The prosecutor had made it clear to us that Paul's actions, his presence on the bridge at that hour, were immaterial to the case. The charge was "failure to give assistance" after an injury, and then lying to police about his damaged car being stolen (public mischief). Perhaps the accused hoped extenuating circumstance would mitigate the sentence?

In the meantime, the Crown planned to have the note examined by a hand-writing analyst and asked for a sample of Paul's writing. Searching through his things, I discovered a card sent by Paul's former girlfriend. Here was the reason I had found the printing on the "suicide note" so familiar. To me, this handwriting looked identical to the note. But why would the girl cooperate in defense of the man accused in Paul's death? Previously, she had expressed nothing but sorrow and love for Paul since his death. Did the girl fancy herself the reason for Paul's death — that he had leapt in front of a car out of a failed love affair? Was the note simply the result of the overactive romantic imagination of a teenage girl? If so, she likely had no idea of its far-reaching effect. I included her card with the handwriting samples and sent them to the prosecutor.

The sentencing was postponed until late September. Attending court that autumn day for the young man involved in the death of our son ranked right up there with some other agonizing milestones we had faced. Police at our door at five a.m. Identifying the body. Ironing a shirt for Paul to be buried in. Fearing that Paul would be found at fault in his death; perhaps even hearing him accused of flinging himself into the path of a car.

As an answer to the prayers of many on our behalf, we were again spared the pain of the Defense suggesting Paul was suicidal. They abandoned entirely the false evidence of a suicide note purportedly written by him. It was a profound relief.

There were other realities to face. Because of the defendant's running from court in January, when the whole case was to have been completed, he had been in Remand since being caught in February. And because of crowded conditions in Remand, time served there can be counted one-and-a-half to two times credit toward whatever he would be sentenced. Added to that, eligibility for parole could be factored in. Subtracting all this from an approximate two-year sentence could mean the young man would be released shortly.

We were aware of this.

That day, we were apprehensive about the possibility of being called on to read the victim impact statements we wrote prior to the opening of the case in January. Back then, we had written them from our hearts with attitudes of forgiveness. The legal maneuvers and manipulations since then had sorely tried that conciliatory stance. Yet we knew that because God has forgiven us so much, we are under obligation to forgive those who sin against us. In God's mercy, he both forgave us and took the penalty we deserve. In our forgiveness of others, we bear the pain of their offense but justice requires the penalty still needs to be paid.

Whatever the sentence, it could never restore to us what we have lost. Some have asked why we would want to see the defendant go to prison at all if we have forgiven him. To answer that, we have drawn on scripture and thought long and hard. First, there is a sacredness to human lives. They matter intrinsically. Their worth is not measured by the contribution they make or their value to loved ones. Because human life – Paul's life – matters, our society and justice system must in some way recognize the value of that life. Second, there is right and wrong. God has declared it and each of us knows it intuitively. Even the youngest child shrieks when something is taken from him. It is right that there be some penalty for actions that cause a death, and if that cannot be determined, at least the carelessness and deceit afterward must be punished.

That day we were trusting God for a legal recognition of the intrinsic value of our son's life. We knew that whatever sentence was given and whatever time was ultimately served, it would never come close to reflecting Paul's true value. For now, in this life, we would have to be content with that. But some sort of penalty would tell the world that human life has inherent worth.

Chapter 36 – A Dad's Perspective

On September 30, 2015, Court of Queen's Bench opened for the sentencing of the man who struck and killed our son October 6, 2012. It was exactly three years to the day that we had last seen Paul alive. That had been a Sunday evening and we were celebrating my husband's birthday at Tony Roma's restaurant. Paul had ordered a large chicken burger, I remember.

Court began with our victim impact statements prior to sentencing.

A victim impact statement is a relatively new development in court, instituted as a reaction to court cases focusing too much on the accused. It is a way to remind the public and the court of the very real and lasting damage a crime has inflicted on both the victim and his family and friends. It must be written prior to the beginning of court, sealed, and only opened the day of sentencing. We were instructed to refrain from commenting on the evidence in the case and focus on how the crime has affected our lives. We had also been told it could affect the sentence.

Here is what my husband wrote in late December 2014, prior to the opening of the case in January. During the reading of this statement, the accused hung his head, weeping.

"The first thing I want to say is to the accused and his family. I understand that this tragic event is a tragedy for you as well. No one expects that these things will happen. Like us, your lives are profoundly changed. I sympathize with you. In fact, when I was awakened at five a.m. that terrible morning to a policeman demanding to know if my son was at home, I at first feared that one of my own sons had done some terrible thing. I do not envy the position you're in. I've known the comfort of those who have shared my grief. I suspect that you've not experienced the same kind of support. Please accept my heartfelt sympathies.

"Moving forward, both our families will have the tragic memory of this whole terrible thing… It will always be with us. There is a difference though and that is that you get to continue with your life. That's a luxury Paul does not have. The lives of our family members are forever changed. You, despite this tragedy, still have the hope of the pleasure of one another's company… You have a future to look forward to. My birthday which was the Sunday prior to Paul's death will be forever tainted by the fact that it was the last time I saw Paul alive. The Thanksgiving holiday will always bear the memory of the weekend my son was killed. Never again will I look around the table at my family and see Paul included among those I love. My heart breaks when I think of the day my twin granddaughters will look at the photo of Paul holding them as very young children and ask, 'who is this that's holding us?' They will be told that's your Uncle Paul and they will ask 'where is he?'

"I'm frequently reminded of how helpless I felt that morning when I phoned my daughter Becky, the mother of these two little ones and gave her this news. I remember the heart-wrenching, uncontrollable sobbing on the other end of the line… all that distance, way down in Texas where I could not comfort her. Becky, though a young girl herself, had helped much with the care of Paul as a baby and had been a close friend to him in later years. My heart was wrenched again when I later heard about how Paul's brother Jonathan, with whom he'd been staying, had wept in agony, alone, after I called him with the news. As I listened to him describe his anguish and understood how alone he felt at that time it was almost more than I could bear. Jonny and Paul had been best friends their whole lives.

"Paul's youngest brother Timothy has Down syndrome and even though he was fifteen at the time of Paul's death, he is very much like a younger child. I cannot express how difficult it was to sit down with him that morning and explain that the police had come and told us that Paul had been killed and that he would not be coming home again. How much did he understand? I don't know. A few days later when the police came again to our home, Timothy ran and hid until they left. I asked him why he had done that and he said, 'I don't want it to happen.'

"'What?' I asked.

"'Die,' he replied. I had to help him understand that the police came only to tell us what had happened, not that they had killed his brother.

"In the months and through the winter following Paul's death, after the cards and calls stopped coming, I began to struggle with depression which continues even now. I would go out in the dark early morning to feed our sheep and chickens and be reminded that this had been Paul's work. Now, not only do I not have him to help but with each thing I do that he formerly did, I'm reminded of the loss… the death of my son. Everywhere I look around home, I see something that reminds me of him. There are frequent tears, even now. The winter seemed so long and so hard and I felt so heavy. I wondered what it's really all for. Why continue? Then with the approach of spring, I was filled with a new anxiety because I saw it as the closing of a chapter, of somehow moving on, without Paul. The anniversary of his death felt much the same way. The grief was somewhat different, almost more intense. The shock that allowed me to efficiently deal with all the details in the early days, was now gone and I was left with only the pain.

"The general feeling of despondency and pessimism that I now carry with me has a negative effect on my relationships and my performance at work. I lack enthusiasm for the things that would usually interest me. Even as I write this, I struggle. I've shared numerous thoughts here but have in no way exhausted the recounting of the effects this tragedy has had on my life. There is much more that could be said. I don't feel the energy to put it into words and am aware that this is already long.

"And in it all I'm haunted by the question; would Paul still be alive if the driver had remained at the scene and gotten help? I will always wonder about that."

Chapter 37 – Our Day in Court

My stomach churned as I anticipated reading my own statement in court. We'd been offered the option of reading our statements ourselves, having them read to the court or read only by the judge, the prosecutor, the defense counsel and the defendant himself. I recalled the conciliatory attitude I'd held while writing mine nine months previous. There had been enough twists in the case to test our patience. The animosity I'd sensed from the defendant's father had tempted me to alter my view. How much worse would it have been if Paul's death had resulted from a deliberate act? And how much more would my willingness to forgive be tried if the perpetrator had been openly jeering and defiant as I'd read of in other cases? I reminded myself this was nothing like that.

Because my husband had chosen to read his statement in court, I would too. This was our one chance to speak for Paul publicly, he later told me. I felt the same way. Here is what I said:

"What impact does the death of a teenage son have? How does it affect a family?

"In order to function, you must always set aside a vital part of yourself. Otherwise, everything is a reminder of the boy you once had and now don't. And everything makes you cry.

"From the kitchen spices that he'd use to generously sprinkle on the breakfast sandwiches he made for his little brother and himself … to the couch he always sat on, watching movies with us … to the places in your memory that picture so vividly the chattering little boy he once was, busy researching jewels or writing down codes and serial numbers in his notebook titled: Plans for World Domination … to his red guitar so silent now… All the ordinary things of his life hold a painful significance.

"Christmas and holidays bring our family together but always with a hole, unfillable by any other person. The nieces he loved so much will grow up not remembering him and his new nephew will never meet him. In the line-up of five handsome groomsmen at his older brother's wedding last summer, the place that should have been Paul's was filled by a friend. But it's always a gap to us.

"After the initial shock of being awakened at 4:55 a.m. by the police at your door with terrible, incomprehensible news – something that fills every subsequent night waking with images of flashing lights – you learn to settle down to the reality of permanent loss.

But it's that very permanence, first noticeable when you lay your unrecognizable son in his coffin, then when you see his name and dates carved irrevocably on his headstone that carries with it the monumental pain.

"You get over the first confused expectation that surely he'll come home with his brothers for the weekends, but as his friends begin to graduate from college and get married, you realize every milestone of life they experience you'll be thinking of what might have been for your son.

The most painful thing for me in the face of the permanent loss of our son has been the questions for which in this life there will never be an answer.

"What would he have become? How would he have used his considerable intellect and musical gifts?

"Once he got past the stage where it was so hard to express deeply personal views, what would he have said about life and God, love and family? Would he have given us, as parents, commendation for how we raised him, as his siblings have? Did he know how much we loved him?

"And where is he now? Did he clearly understand and trust that when God's Son Jesus was so cruelly executed more than two thousand years ago, he was the substitute, taking the penalty for Paul's sin?

"It's because of Jesus and the promise he brought for life after this life that we have the assurance these questions will one day be answered.

"In the meantime, the name of C. is now permanently linked to our family. As I have prayed for him and his family and will continue to do so, I've asked that he understand the extreme seriousness of the loss of a human life. But I also pray he would understand that even though the actions of a moment may have life-and-death consequences, there can be forgiveness from God and others when there is genuine repentance. I pray he would experience that and would live the rest of his life, recognizing it as a gift from God and honouring him in it."

Chapter 38 – Sentence is Passed

Much legal mumbo jumbo followed our victim impact statements as the prosecution and defense discussed the few case precedents set in Canada for the relatively new law regarding "failure to give assistance".

When C.'s newly-appointed defense lawyer rose to make his case, he first turned to us and on behalf of his client, expressed condolences for our loss. He said nothing that happened in court that day would make up for that loss. He noted that we appeared to be people of faith and hoped that our faith would be a comfort to us. I was touched… briefly.

"The responsibility for the events of October 6, 2012," the defense lawyer continued, "began long before the collision. The offenses charged did not cause Paul's death." Then he turned to the judge and began to make his case for the immediate release of his client. Essentially, as I had feared, he blamed Paul for having been on the bridge.

Apparently, it's common practice prior to sentencing for the defense to describe mitigating circumstances and the accused's background. He explained that the accused was an only child, adopted as an infant, bright and accomplished. He'd attained Grade Eight Conservatory standing in piano, graduated from high school and attended college one year. As a teen he'd struggled with depression and his parents thought it might be helpful if he met his birth family. Living with that family for six months led him to an addiction. His parents then sent him to rehab where he overcame his mental illness and addiction. From there he came to Alberta to work in the oil patch, impressing his boss with his work. While in jail since February of 2015, he had at times been triple bunked and had suffered much from post-traumatic stress.

The defense argued that time served under such crowded and difficult circumstances (commonly counted one-and-a-half to two times the period) amounted to almost a one-year sentence and therefore, the accused had already served the necessary time.

The judge next asked the defendant if he would like to address the court.

I was surprised at how quickly C. rose and said he wanted to do so. He turned toward us with what seemed sincerity and said, "I am so sorry for my mistake... Paul will be a name I never forget." I noticed he called it a mistake, not taking responsibility for killing someone, even accidentally.

Then he continued. It was as though the first part was prepared. Defense lawyers advise their clients that showing remorse in court can translate into leniency in sentencing. But the second half seemed to be a direct response to having read and heard our victim impact statements.

"I'm very thankful," he said, with some fervency, "to hear your voices and what you had to say ... I will always remember Paul and the Bertin family." He said more along that line but what stood out to me was his sincerity. Noticeable by its absence, however, was any request for our forgiveness.

Court that day had a different atmosphere. It seemed even the defense lawyer was less adversarial. The young man's parents appeared subdued; there was a slight slump to his father's shoulders. Perhaps they were more resigned?

When the judge returned with his verdict, he used the words of other judges in similar cases, describing the actions of leaving an injured person as "deplorable".

The accused, the judge said, was solely responsible for the accident and subsequent offenses. He made "a conscious decision to leave the scene and left a dying man on the bridge alone to suffer the indignity of being run over a second time, something that wouldn't have happened had Mr. C. remained."

The young man was sentenced to twenty-eight months, less two months for remorse expressed in court. In addition, he would be subject to a two-year driving ban following his release and was ordered to give a DNA sample. The judge said he did not feel obligated to give full one-and-a-half times credit for time served. He noted it was the defendant's fault he'd been in provincial jail since February for having run away from court in January. There was, however, no time added for that misdemeanor. A thirty-day sentence for the public mischief charge of lying to police about his car being stolen was to be served concurrently.

Was this then the value society placed on our son's life? A living eternal soul equivalent to twenty-six months' incarceration? How paltry a price it seemed!

"I knew that whatever happened would in no way approximate the loss and grief we've experienced," my husband later said. "My head knew that but my heart was expecting something. I didn't know what. It was like the times I feel so compelled to visit Paul's grave. Yet when I do, there's nothing that satisfies that compulsion."

I understand the reaction of victims' families when they come out of a courtroom angry at injustice. If their hope is that somehow their family member's death will be atoned for, they will always be disappointed. Even a death penalty can't satisfy for the loss of a loved one. However, we went into court fully aware there would be no more than a two- to three-year sentence. As far as man's justice was able, justice had been served. The legal system can only address what can be proven beyond reasonable doubt — and for all our sakes, we want it to be that way. A human judge can never judge the state of a man's heart, or his thoughts and intentions if he doesn't disclose them.

Perhaps one of the most important things we've been robbed of because of C. fleeing the scene that night is the full story. We can't know exactly where Paul was walking because of C.'s lying about the accident. We're left with the sad possibility that he was doing something foolishly risky that led to his death. Yet that might not be so. We also don't know whether Paul moved or said anything as he lay dying. If he was conscious after being struck, we're left with the pain of knowing his final moments were spent without the comfort of human kindness.

But God knows the full truth of what happened that night those years ago. While I rest in the promise of ultimate divine justice, I also shudder. "It is a fearful thing to fall into the hands of the living God" (Hebrews 10:31). I can't wish divine retribution on anyone, and I pray C. will come to God for the forgiveness he so freely and graciously offers all who repent.

Driving home after the sentencing, we experienced a strange, numb emptiness. In a sense it was another severing of ties with Paul, "like burying him a second time," my husband said. While we had court to attend, even with all its twists and turns, we were actively involved on behalf of our son. Once that was settled, there was nothing more we could do for him.

"I now feel I no longer have a legitimate reason to talk about the loss of my son," Mike later wrote. It was a bleak finality.

Chapter 39 – God Rules over Evil

I have never thought God was punishing us for our sin by taking our son. "We should not view the death of Christians as a punishment from God or in any way a result of a penalty due to us for our sins," writes theologian Wayne Grudem. Nor have I been angry with God, as though somehow, he had no right to have allowed such a thing. Many people are. Why aren't I?

I can't claim any great faith or superior knowledge. But I do know that over time, as I gained a greater understanding of the sovereignty of God and the doctrines of his grace, my trust in him has increased. He is God and I'm not. There is amazing rest in that truth. I can trust Jesus who describes himself as both the giver and the taker of life.

> *'Now see that I, even I, am He,*
> *And there is no God besides Me;*
> *I kill and I make alive;*
> *I wound and I heal;*

Nor is there any who can deliver from My hand."
(Deuteronomy 32:39)

"Settle this in your heart," John Piper has tweeted. "Life is a gift from God. He owes it to none. He may take it at any age, anytime, and do no wrong."

Something as large as life or death is far beyond anything a mother can control. The Bible tells us that our times are in God's hands. "And in your book they all were written, the days fashioned for me, when as yet there were none of them." (Psalm 139:16)

When Job's ten children were killed in a cyclone, he said, "Naked I came from my mother's womb and naked shall I return there. The Lord gave and the Lord has taken away; blessed be the name of the Lord" (Job 1:21).

In December 2004, a colossal tsunami devastated Thailand and other parts of southeast Asia. Shortly after, I heard of one irreligious Canadian man who uncharacteristically began donating to charity. He also phoned his daughter, my friend, and surprised her by expressing his love for her. Something about these giant acts of nature, far beyond our control, puts the fear of God into us. We come face to face with raw, unbridled Omnipotence and, by contrast, our own sinfulness.

A look at our insurance policies reveals our human recognition that natural disasters are acts of God. Isaac Watts, writer of the hymn *I Sing the Mighty Power of God* expressed it this way:

"And clouds arise and tempests blow
By order from His throne."

Yes, it's fearsome to contemplate the kind of astounding power that can devastate the earth and the people who live on it. It inevitably leads to serious questions about God's love and goodness. I tend to think God is like me; that unlimited power inevitably leads to corruption and evil. But he's not. He's perfectly loving and perfectly just. It's only that my finite mind can't fathom how any good can come out of evil or devastation.

"Sometimes we make the foolish assumption that our heavenly Father has no right to insist that we trust Him unless He makes His infinite wisdom completely understandable to us," Randy Alcorn wrote, significantly, on October 5, 2012, the day before Paul's death. "What we call the problem of evil is often the problem of our finite and fallen understanding."

Psalm 136 repeats the line, "His lovingkindness endures forever," twenty-six times. That works out to once for every letter of our alphabet – you might say it encompasses every word in the English language. Could the repetition be necessary because I don't really believe it or trust God's love? Could my doubt about God's goodness reveal more about who I am than it reflects on his character? He is not cruel and evil. He is perfectly just and at the same time perfectly good. Like any parent, God presses these truths into my forgetful, distrusting head by repetition. Disasters, suffering and evil are often cited as a reason for *not* believing in God.

In *Emergency: True Stories from the Nation's ERs*, an emergency room physician stands over the bedside of a beautiful, blond four-year-old boy, drowned in a swimming pool. He tells the parents there is nothing more to be done and he will have to allow the child's heart to stop beating.

The parents ask for just a few more moments in which to say goodbye. As the mother chokes back sobs, the father, in broken tones, commits his son's soul to God. The doctor silently listens, resisting the man's faithful acceptance of what has happened. He writes:

> *"Stop this insanity!" I wanted to yell. "There is no reason and no justification for your child to have died. None whatever…There is nothing good about any of this.*
>
> *"Why are you holding back your tears, and your fury?" I went on, screaming at them inside my brain. "Your little boy is dead! No god would have stolen him, nor will any give him back. This is the world we live in, and even an eternity in heaven, if it really existed, couldn't atone for this suffering."*

This doctor, devoted to saving lives, yet who witnesses death on a daily basis, cries out against the unnatural, abhorrent, ugly reality. He "rages against the dying of the light." But do you hear what he's saying? In his anguish he rightly rails against the cruelty of the world we live in. Yet at the same time he wants to rob the parents of any hope of another, better world. He wants them to stop holding back their tears and anger and offers to replace them with – what? His own, somehow more reasonable anger arising from hopelessness, despair, nihilism?

In his book, *The Rage Against God,* journalist and author Peter Hitchens recounts his announcement at the age of twelve that he didn't believe in God. His headmaster "avoided arguments and made a mild riposte about how the deaths of those I loved might later alter my view, which I scorned at the time but which I never forgot and later found to be accurate." It is our helplessness in the face of death's inevitability that brings the recognition we are not, in fact, the captain of our fate. And if we're not, we instinctively know, Someone else is.

Some Christians attempt to defend God's honour by saying God has nothing to do with the tragedy or suffering we undergo. Suffering, they say, is brought to us by Satan or by our own sin, never by God. But then, where does that leave God? Looking the other way? Helpless to do anything about it? As author and pastor David Platt says, "that's terrible news. It means He's not in control and can't ensure trials will be used for our good."

I find no comfort in the line of reasoning that distances God from the pain and tragedy of our lives. In fact, it's utterly frightening to consider alternatives to God's being perfectly in control and ordering all things from his throne. Is God not at all in control of the events of this life? Or is he partially in control but somehow dependent on the actions and intentions of man? It seems to me there are only three other options as to who governs the affairs of life. If it's not God who ordains tragic events to occur, are they simply caused by the weakness, faulty thinking and selfish motives of human beings? Is Satan, that malevolent personification and source of evil, the sole reason bad things happen? Or do tragedies, evil and suffering happen randomly? If any of these are true, evil wins. And the idea of evil being in control of anything, let alone our son's life is an unbearable prospect.

The Bible teaches that evil and suffering are ordained by God. Notice I said *ordained* and not *caused.* One of the clearest statements of God's use of men's evil deeds for his purposes is found in Genesis 50:19. A young man's brothers hated him and conspired to sell him into slavery. He suffered for years before rising to a top government position. Years after their wicked deed, he met them again and told them, "You meant it for evil against me; but God meant it for good."

God prescribes birth defects and disabilities too: "Who has made man's mouth? Or who makes the mute, the deaf, the seeing, or the blind? Have not I, the Lord?" (Exodus 4:11) He has power over life and death: "Now see that I, even I, am He, And there is no God besides Me; I kill and I make a live; I wound and I heal." (Deuteronomy 32:39) At times he even wants certain people to die:

"…They did not heed the voice of their father, because the Lord desired to kill them." (I Samuel 2:25) Most memorably, God's absolute reign is shown in the worst evil ever perpetrated in this world, the worst suffering ever endured. God's perfect Son was betrayed and murdered by sinful humanity and it was all part of God's long-established plan.

"For truly against Your holy Servant Jesus, whom You anointed, both Herod and Pontius Pilate, with the Gentiles and the people of Israel, were gathered together *to do whatever Your hand and Your purpose determined before to be done.*" (Acts 4:27, 28, italics mine)

The absolute kingly rule of God that I had so feared early in 2012, I now clung to as my precious comfort and hope. Only if a loving God had ordained this tragedy could there be any higher purpose for it. He promises his people two things during suffering.

First, He has promised to be with me in the midst of the sorrow. Jesus was even called a Man of Sorrows to prove his entering into the pain of this life with us.

Years earlier, I wrote about an incident with one of our other sons that in a small way illustrated these truths for me.

July 24, 1992 – Our two-year-old had to have surgery to correct a congenital defect. It was heart-wrenching to release him to the OR nurse. But the recovery was more difficult still, since he couldn't understand some of the routine we needed to follow for his care.

Due to an error the doctor made, an unexpected follow-up surgery was required two weeks later. In a few days, we returned to the hospital to remove the stitches. By this time my son was catching on that this place meant pain. When the doctor came out to talk to me in the waiting room, my little boy clung tightly to me in recognition of the man.

A nurse offered to take him into the consulting room where the doc would take out the stitches. But the uncomprehending fear in my boy's eyes, made me choose to take him in and stay with him myself. It would have been easier to let the nurse hold him down as he thrashed and flailed, screaming, while the doctor worked. It would have been less painful to me not to have to look into his terrified eyes. Or feel him struggle against my tight hold as I tried to prevent him inflicting a worse pain on himself by his resistance. I wish I had never had to sense in those eyes the accusation of betrayal. *Why are you doing this? Why won't you rescue me? Why are you so cruel?*

But I could not leave him alone in his time of trial. I loved him. And though he couldn't understand, I was allowing it for his ultimate good, to spare him more pain in the short-term and to ensure him a good life in the future. I was with him in it. And loving him. My tears fell onto his face and mingled with his.

> *"In all their affliction He was afflicted,*
> *And the angel of His presence saved them;*
> *In His love and in His pity, He redeemed them;*
> *And He bore them and carried them*
> *All the days of old." (Isaiah 63:9)*

Second, God has promised to use suffering to work his perfect plan. "The Lord uses sorrowful tragedy to set the stage for surprising triumph – whether in this life or the life to come," Platt says.

Someday, though perhaps not in this life, that plan will cause me to gasp in amazement at the intricacy of his foresight. I'll leap for joy at his genius. "For this light momentary affliction, is preparing for us an eternal weight of glory beyond all comparison." (II Corinthians 4:17, ESV)

"The only way I can say it's light, momentary affliction," says pastor Matt Chandler, of his brain cancer, "is if I have a ten-thousand-year perspective." And taking the view of millennia will allow us to appreciate the stunning reality of being in the very presence of God, dimming our recall of pain to a distant memory and engulfing our minds with joy.

This is the only answer that makes sense to me on the question of why a good God allows suffering.

Chapter 40 – Grief – A Constant Companion

In those early weeks after the funeral, it seemed everyone who offered condolences also shared a tale of untimely death. An eighteen-year-old sister, killed with friends in a car wreck just weeks before high school graduation. A toddler son, crushed by the tractor driven by his own father. A teenage grandson dying alone in a field when a loaded pickup truck rolled onto him. A still-born baby, still grieved more than thirty years later. A young husband, murdered in a robbery for five bucks and a pack of smokes. Clearly, these folks understood our sorrow. Their stories introduced me to a subterranean world of grief where private pain seeks an outlet to the surface. In case I hadn't recognized it before, I saw that in this life, everyone suffers. Everyone, it seemed, had lost a young family member. I realized, too, that every death is tragic, not just the death of the young. After all, in the light of eternity, even ninety years is a mere blip on time's monitor. Though I'd never signed up for the bereaved mother label, I found myself thrust into the company of many tender-hearted souls. Grief shared was easier to bear.

None of these fellow-mourners, however, could have known they were only one of a growing list of tragedies piling up in my mind. Around that time, too, I read the obituary of a local ninety-one-year-old lady. The list of family members who had predeceased her stunned me. Her parents, eight older siblings and their spouses, two husbands, nephews, several children, a grandson and even a great-grandchild — she'd grieved the death of all of them. Would the rest of my life hold nothing but more sorrow and loss? So many tragedies! So much misery! The weight of suffering accumulated to an almost unbearable burden.

In fact, I became accustomed to expecting loss in everyone's life. When prayer requests would come for those suffering serious injury or illness, I was surprised when the sufferer *didn't* die. And it came as a surprise, when I later attended friends' fiftieth wedding anniversary event, that all their children, children's spouses, grandchildren and their mates, and great-grandchildren were still living.

A peculiar torment for me was meeting new people and being asked about our children. Was it lying to say we had seven? Folks asked the question to make conversation, not to hear a raw tale of woe. But I couldn't stop the years-old habit of counting to seven; couldn't simply cut Paul out of our family as though he'd never been. The truth was, we had raised seven; the deeper truth was that the one we had lost was still living, only in a different dimension.

There are many guides on how to help the bereaved, and I'd concur with all their wisdom — send cards, especially including memories of the deceased, be a listening ear, help in practical ways, remember the critical anniversaries yet to come. In the time before and after the funeral, we had folks who willingly took away our garbage, and others who washed all the windows in our house. Some donated money to help our children come home for the funeral, while still others offered hospitality to our out-of-town guests. These were priceless gifts to us.

Another piece of advice we found true was, don't avoid mention of the deceased even if it evokes tears. "I want to remember more, not less," Mike said. "People talk about healing but does healing mean that I forget? Does it mean I stop caring, stop loving, stop missing Paul? How can healing be desirable if that's the case?"

We learned too, that there are special temptations in grief – becoming self-absorbed, snapping at people, attributing bad motives to others, assuming no one has suffered like I have, that no one understands. It was tempting to use grief as an excuse for bad behaviour. It was too easy to compare "Most Insensitive Comforter" stories. But all it took for me to forgive clumsy attempts at comfort was to recall my own inept words or actions over the years to others who were grieving. Death is such a cataclysm, no one really knows how to help or what to say.

In 1984, Wilma Derksen's daughter, Candace, was found murdered in Winnipeg after a two-month search for the missing thirteen-year-old. In picking up the pieces of their lives, Derksen writes of the difficulty of choosing something as simple as a family movie. To her, it seemed so many touched on the theme of a missing or murdered girl. We were deluged with such triggers too. I'd never been aware of how many movies are rife with hit and run fatalities or the death of a son.

Wilma and her husband, Cliff, found themselves highly sensitive to people's glib talk. "'I could have murdered him' doesn't mean a thing – usually – but with us standing there, it took on real meaning."

We, too, found words and phrases that under normal circumstances would have passed unnoticed, shattering our careful façade. Often, they were words we spoke ourselves. One of us would repeat a family quip coined by Paul. Rosy-cheeked from napping while his dad and brothers slaved in the summer sun, tearing apart our old deck, he was just a little tyke when he came out to survey the work and said, "Look how much we've done!"

Nor does death come with an Idiot's Guide to Mourning. At first, I kept thinking, *if I can just get past this…* But grief isn't like labour and delivery where a few hours of agony are followed by a wonderful outcome. It's not even like a root canal that eventually ends, deadening the pain. I hated the anesthetized sensation of not being able to feel, but at the same time, I dreaded the intermittent moments of sharp sorrow even more. When I was told, "you never get over it," it had seemed the most disheartening thing I could hear. And yet, there is truth in it. What I was yet to learn is that you get stronger to bear it.

In our case, there was an added factor that increased our sense of loss. Paul's death coincided with the emptying of our nest.

"We were given seven wonderful children," my husband said. "They all arrived in just a few short years and for a long time we were a crowd. I was defined by my family, the father of 'all those kids.' When they began to leave home, they left about as quickly as they came. As I think back on the best, most optimistic years of my life, it was the time when we were all together."

That shift in identity was something particularly upsetting to me. For years I had been the home-schooling mom of many — now I was a bereaved mom. It was a label I'd never signed up for.

I resisted this new realm of grieving by escaping into normal life. I clung to routine. Things needed to stay the same. I took our youngest son to theatre practice and volunteered for backstage duty. I sewed for the needy with church women. I wanted to keep our life whole, not quaked into a chasm separating "before" from "after." I worked on my long-shelved novel, but even there, tragic elements and memories of Paul intruded, writing themselves into the manuscript – Paul's grinning dog made an appearance, a straying punk son caused heartache to the main character. The problem was, normal life was fraught with land-mines – hidden, explosive reminders of who we had been and now were no longer. And even if I could dodge those, the stricken, sympathetic looks of people I would meet blasted my illusions.

I didn't want to grieve, much less know how. Is displaying strong emotion the highest and best way to prove the depth of my loss? Is the length or strength of my crying the ultimate measure of my love for my lost loved one? Do screaming or wailing or refusing to eat or to see anyone for weeks or months show more love? Are there better or worse responses to tragedy?

"Maybe death is supposed to be hard," author Joni Eareckson Tada suggests. "Maybe it's supposed to be a taste of hell…If the 'wages of sin is death' I wonder if God has in mind for us to feel — really feel — a little of what the Saviour bore. Or perhaps God wants to remind us of what sin would have earned us, had it not been for Christ."

The Sawi people of Papua New Guinea were brutally honest about death's hideous reality. They used to allow a corpse several days to rot in the rain forest. Then to show their grief and devotion to the departed, family members would plunge their hands into the innards and eat some of the decomposing flesh. Given the unnatural tearing of soul from body that death is, such a horrifying practice may be truly more appropriate.

Only after missionaries brought the Sawi hope for life beyond death did the practice end. Christ's promise of resurrection for those who trust in him transformed their grieving by giving them hope for life after life. It's that hope which is the basis for the controlled, mild approach to death that prevails in western culture.

But as our culture slides further away from its Christian underpinnings, memorial services and "celebrations of life" without that vital foundation are simply a pretense to sanitize and deny the enemy Death. Resurrection, by contrast, offers victory and true hope. The confidence that we will see our loved ones again someday, that death and sorrow will finally end — these are what keep us from despair. I suppose a calm, quiet response to loss could be seen as disinterest, lack of caring, denial or even a time bomb of numbness that will ultimately explode into a breakdown of unbridled emotion. Or it could be evidence of trust in God and his sovereign ways amid distressing tragedy.

Once normal life resumed, I received several comments that I seemed to be "handling" grief very well. I wondered briefly whether I was doing it right. I worried about whether I seemed cold or unfeeling. Oddly, this was a difference between my husband and me; I was calm while he struggled to maintain his composure. There's a common misconception that divorce statistics following the death of a child are disturbingly high — as great as 75%. But a Montana State University study of bereaved parents and divorce found the high number is an urban legend. "Only 9% of respondents divorced following their child's death. 24% of the remaining respondents had considered divorce but had not actually done so. Instead of serving as a catalyst to separate, it would seem that a child's death can actually serve to draw couples together," the authors of the study discovered.

There were some ways in which I believe we had been prepared for tragedy. According to a longitudinal study of bereaved parents published by the U.S. National Institute of Health, "The only significant predictor of a lower likelihood of marital disruption was greater religious participation." My husband and I had a bedrock understanding that God is both good and sovereign, that he is completely free to do as he pleases. God did not owe us any reward for past good deeds. In fact, if we got what we deserved we would never have lived. We also understood that, because of sin, suffering is an integral part of life on this earth. God's purpose for us was not to make us healthy and wealthy. We knew not to ask, "Why me?" In fact, given the relative ease of life in North America compared with the rest of the world a more logical question is, "Why not me?" Even so, I had learned, as Martha Nicholson's poem described, "He never gives a thorn without this added grace: He takes the thorn to pin aside the veil which hides His face." Suffering was intended to cause us to cling tighter to Jesus. And best of all, we knew that this life is not all there is.

Two other practices also helped prevent a break up: We talked about Paul and our grief freely and often, and still do. And we followed the advice of an older gentleman in our church who had known a similar loss, *don't blame each other*. It would have been easy. We knew each other's faults only too well. But neither of us ever went there.

Perhaps the friends who saw me handling grief well were observing numbness. It took many months for the full impact of Paul's death to make its aching passage from my mind to my soul. Eventually, I was to learn there was no right or wrong way to mourn. It was not something done on display or for the benefit of others. And though grief changes us in unforeseen, permanent ways, there are stages, there is healing and there is comfort.

As for my ability to keep on with day-to-day living, keep trusting in God, keep "handling grief" – I give credit only to him. Only he could keep me from despair. At first, I sought hope in answers to questions that, in this life, must remain unanswered. But steadily, he kept drawing me back to himself as the answer I need, the only basis for hope. Like Abraham wanting tangible proof that God would answer his prayers the way he expected, I had wanted beyond-doubt certainty that Paul was now in heaven. And like his answer to Abraham thousands of years ago, God's assurance to me has been himself. "Do not be afraid, I am your shield, your exceedingly great reward" (Genesis 15:1). If our son's eternal destiny is not one of those things for me to know for certain, my confidence in anything in this life or the next is based on God's promises and his perfect character. The far greater question than what has become of Paul is, what kind of God is God? The Bible reveals him to be gracious, pardoning abundantly! I do believe that Paul is safe with Jesus, having the time of his life. But if it turns out I'm wrong, I will still be able to say the Judge of all the earth has done right (Genesis 18:25). As the Heidelberg catechism states, the knowledge of God's providence means I can be patient when things go against me, thankful when things go well, and for the future I can have good confidence in my faithful God and Father that nothing will separate me from his love.

This unshakable confidence doesn't mean I don't grieve. Just that I don't grieve as though there is no hope. Grief ambushes me when I least expect it. Startling reminders of Paul assail me at the most inopportune times. I walk down the beverage aisle in the grocery store and catch a glimpse of the lime cordial Paul insisted I buy for him, and the tears start. Half a can of black olives stays in the fridge for over a year – he's the only one of the family who liked them and I can't bear to throw them out. Odd things trigger memories. I phone a neighbour and struggle to compose myself before she answers – the last two digits of her number are the year of Paul's birth. The pie recipe book flops open to the page for Key Lime Pie, something Paul concocted on his own for himself and his dad while I was away.

In the spring of 2013, I was in Texas for a few weeks with my daughter and her family, after the birth of their first son. At church one Sunday I was blindsided by the song sung at Paul's funeral. It was only the second time I'd heard it since then. As it always does the music washed waves of emotion over me. It promised life and joy and peace with the final heartbeat of the sinner who trusts in Jesus.

I sobbed as quietly as I could while, without a tissue or even a sleeve, I mopped up tears with the hem of my skirt. The church musicians had no way of knowing the next day would have been Paul's nineteenth birthday.

Chapter 41 – Good out of Evil?

Did any good come out of our tragedy? In the first days, I sought the answer desperately but came up empty. A random thought suggested Paul, with his innate intellect, might have become an influence for unbelief in this world had he lived. Had God taken him before he became hardened in his rejection of God? It was hardly a comforting line of thought.

There are some results I must agree are good. My reserved husband is much freer to tell our children of his love for them. Our relationships with all our children are closer.

The woman who first found Paul on the street told me he'd changed her life, impressing on her the need to spend more time with her children, presumably because of the impact of his shortened life. The passenger in the car that struck Paul testified that she "used to drink quite heavily," leading me to hope that as a direct result of the death of our son, she did not do so now.

During the court case, a young friend of Paul's from the punk community wrote this in response to the blog posts I had published about it:

"Hi Eleanor; Just wanted to send a quick message and let you know that you and your family have been on my heart and mind a lot the last few weeks. I've been reading the articles you have written and they're extremely difficult to read, but I just want you to know that I respect and commend your strength and way with words and I'm sure I'm not alone. Paul's life and death had an incredible effect on so many people (as I'm sure you know and deeply understand) and the way you and your family have dealt with this has impacted me personally in a huge way..."

Not knowing what she meant about Paul's life and death having an incredible effect on so many leaves me guessing. I appreciate her kind sympathy, but I wish for more specific explanations. At least her note shows me there was some sort of impact. And I'm only now, years later, learning that some things lodge in one's mind, planting a seed that may bear future fruit. Likewise, new evidence can turn up long after a tragedy, that alters the way we view an event. Twenty years ago, a friend's older sister was killed in a car struck by a train. Only recently, my friend discovered that her sister had actually died in a heroic attempt to rescue others in the vehicle when she herself could have been saved.

Two-and-a-half years after Paul's death I was jarred alert by a television ad touting a new feature on the very make of car that struck and killed my son. The Subaru would now be equipped with technology that could detect an object or figure in front of it, immediately and automatically stopping the vehicle to avoid collision! Anguish clutched at my soul as I watched the ad. The technology came two years too late to save my boy. Yet I should be glad for anything that could prevent another family from experiencing the loss we have.

And what about me? Has the death of Paul brought any good in my heart? I know it has. I have gained a far more compassionate heart for the parents of prodigals and for the families of crime victims. My first reaction to that sort of bad news used to be to find some fault in the victim. The person hadn't been raised right. They should not have been involved in questionable activities. They shouldn't have been present in dangerous locations, accompanying the wrong sort of crowd. These are the kinds of reactions we have when we're seeking to assure ourselves such a thing will never happen to us or to those we love. Simple cause and effect; input equals output. But not anymore.

Now my first thought is *that could have been me.* Who among us has not gone astray? Now, too, I think of the pain experienced by those left behind. Interviewed on television after the murder of her two-year-old daughter, there's little trace of that pain yet in the voice and face of a young mother — her calm demeanor, the matter-of-fact way she answers reporters' questions. I don't judge her. *She doesn't get it yet!* But she will, I know. And I pray when the horrible reality comes home to her at last, she will turn to the Creator of her baby, who himself saw his Son murdered.

I've learned children must be raised in faith, not fear. Parents must trust God with the outcome of their efforts to train their kids. It's a truth I knew, but forgot, faced with the giants of rebellion and resistance. I no longer fear the symptoms of those giants. At a wedding in 2014, I forced myself away from my own friends and relatives, turning toward a young couple, he with an outstanding mohawk, she with fuchsia hair. I greeted them and asked the young man about his suit-jacket — two vertical halves of different jackets whip-stitched together down the back. He seemed pleased with the attention, describing his process in detail. He even laughed at my predictable quip that he had another jacket at home just like that one. My bitterness toward the punk scene has dissolved.

"I believe that many rock lyricists think they are screaming at God, when they are really screaming out for Him," writes rock star-turned-Christian, Alice Cooper. I've returned to the truth that like me, everyone needs God's love and mercy, no matter what their struggle or appearance.

Recently, I found a photo of Paul and his cousin as young children, dressed as bride and groom. I placed it with the wedding pictures of our other children in a photo frame bearing the caption, "Every time I think of you, I give thanks to my God." The caption made me realize that for years, I had not been thanking God for Paul. But now I carry with me that reminder to give thanks for Paul's life. It's given me new eyes, grateful eyes. Photos of him show me God gave us a healthy, bright child, full of squinty smiles and creativity. I glance upward to clear the tears from my eyes and see the ceiling drywall he supported while his dad screwed the sheets to the joists. I enjoy the cobblestone garden path for which he dug away the sod. The horizon of the sheep pasture is unobstructed now because of Paul's steady work dragging out and burning dead trees. His idea of mowing down the unsightly patch of weeds of an unused garden area was a good one and I carry on the practice. I find gratitude for him expanding in my heart to push out the bitterness that clawed at me in those early months.

Unexpectedly because of tragedy, I've experienced a greater trust in Jesus, a renewed confidence in prayer. I've learned that God gives prayer prompts *so that* he can answer. And I'm utterly convinced that he will do whatever it takes to save those who are his own. I've learned that even unconsciousness and near-death cannot thwart God's unfailing ability to bring his chosen ones to repentance. He promises to bring his children back to himself. Though the method may be fearsome, still the promise holds.

I'm also more certain of God's love for me. Truly, he makes no mistakes. I've seen that there is joy amid sorrow and that the pain is not constant or unrelieved. I have tested God's promises and found firm footing. He says he will never leave me or forsake me and he has not. He promises to answer prayer and I have seen him do so. He pledges he will be a refuge in sorrow and I have never been without the safety of his comfort.

Whether good has resulted from our son's death is a different question from whether it was worth that good.

When teenaged Candace Derksen was found after two months of dreadful uncertainty that winter of 1984-85, the family was finally able to hold a funeral. Many young people who had known Candace resolved to live more fervently for Christ. The organization Child Find was launched out of her tragic death. Donations poured in toward a swimming pool for a local summer camp Candace had loved. Most lasting of all, however, was the impact upon members of the media and others who heard of these parents' resolve to forgive. "Peace Triumphs!" the newspaper headlines trumpeted, paying tribute to the Winnipeg family's trust in God and willingness to forgive the perpetrators.

"I looked at the headlines," Wilma writes, "but somehow they weren't enough for me. The pain was still too raw. I needed so much more good to equalize this pain… I wondered if there was ever going to be enough good to satisfy me."

Is the good that has resulted from Paul's death worth it? I confess, I can't feel that it is. Surely there was some less painful way to accomplish these good things. Like Wilma Derksen, I need so much more good to equalize the pain. But maybe we ask the wrong question when we try to balance the scales of suffering against joy.

Could it be that trust in God despite suffering is the very definition of joy? Job, in the biblical account, lost all his belongings and all his children. Yet in the end, God returned all that and more to him. Did it make up for his losses? The only answer we get in the final chapters of the book is the unanswerable: God is God and we are not. The fact that Jesus's resurrected body still bears the scars of his earthly suffering points to how serious he takes the pains and sorrows of life. And yet, we're told "the sufferings of this present time are not worthy to be compared with the glory which shall be revealed in us." (Romans 8:18)

As a medical missionary during Congo's 1964 war for independence, Dr. Helen Roseveare endured repeated brutal rapes and imprisonment. She struggled with the same question: was her agony worth whatever good might come of it? Afterward she learned to change the question.

"It's not, *is it worth it?*" she said in an interview, "it's, *is He worthy?*" Through the tremendous suffering of her life, she said she found God asking her, "Can you thank me for trusting you with this situation even if I never tell you why?"

We often hear that the death of a child is the worst pain imaginable. But how can pain be ranked or rated?

"A man's suffering is similar to the behaviour of gas," Viktor Frankl writes. "If a certain quantity of gas is pumped into an empty chamber, it will fill the chamber completely and evenly, no matter how big the chamber. Thus, suffering completely fills the human soul and conscious mind, no matter whether the suffering is great or little. Therefore, the 'size' of human suffering is absolutely relative."

Loss of a child is surely the worst fear of any parent. We hover over a toddler at the head of a flight of stairs, our arm shoots out by reflex in front of an older child in the front seat of a car upon sudden braking, we wait up anxiously for a past-curfew teen. These are the involuntary marks of devotion embedded in mothers and fathers. Letting go is painful in the normal course of our child's growing independence. But severing the parent-child bond is uniquely physical, particularly for a mother. In the curious, mysterious manner of life, this son or daughter emerged from her own body. The child is a pledge of hope in the future. Untimely death snatches away that hope when it snatches a child. It overturns the natural order of life. Parents are left with a panoramic view of their child's life from beginning to end, but no parent feels equipped to determine its meaning. And without meaning, we are without hope. Not only that, but there is a powerful sense of failure when a human life we've been entrusted with, ends. How, then, can a parent withstand such pain?

The story is told of a Christ-follower, sentenced to death by burning in the great purge of English Protestants of the 1600s. Many believers were fearful they would be next. Would they stand firm, they wondered, shrinking at the excruciating fate that could well be theirs? Some of their number had already renounced Christ under torture. They loved their Lord but could they be faithful even to death? In a final visit with the man slated for the stake, he promised he would give the other believers a sign to reassure them they would be able to bear the pain, that Jesus would be with them to the bitterest end. The terrible day came. The doomed man was bound to the stake with wet ropes. This executioner would not mercifully pile green wood at the base to allow death by smoke inhalation. A pile of seasoned logs and dry kindling was prepared. The fire was lit. Amongst the crowd, the anguished believers cringed. As the flames leapt upward, the onlookers began to smell singed hair and burning flesh. Before their tormented eyes, they saw their brother slowly begin to move. Silently, with flesh melting off him, he raised his arms in signal. Jesus was with him! The stake could be borne!

Of this I am sure: There is a Light in the darkest night of loss. There is hope for joy and life in the future. Peace lies not in trying to figure out the secret will of God. Rather, it's found in knowing who God is — good, loving and mighty to save his people. And no matter what terrors this life sends, they can be borne because Jesus promises to be with us.

Bibliography

Chapter 6: http://punkmusic.about.com/od/punk101/a/punkhistory2.htm

Chapter 7: www.reddeeradvocate.com, Oct. 9, 2012
The Stettler Independent, Oct. 10, 2012

Chapter 9: *The Grand Weaver: How God Shapes Us Through the Events of Our Lives*, Ravi Zacharias; Zondervan, Grand Rapids, MI, 2007

The Invisible Hand, R.C. Sproul; Word Publishing, Dallas, TX, 1996, p.116.

Chapter 10: *Man's Search for Meaning*, Viktor Frankl, Touchstone Publishers; Greenwich, CT, 1984, p. 76

Does Prayer Change Things? Crucial Questions, R.C. Sproul, Reformation Trust, Sanford, FL, 2009

Chapter 12: http://laws-lois.justice.gc.ca/eng/acts/c-46/section-140.html

Chapter 13: quoted in A Quest for Godliness; p. 86.

Chapter 14: *Which None Can Shut*, Reema Goode, Tyndale House Publishers, Carol Stream, IL, 2010.

Letters of C.S. Lewis, ed. by Warnie Lewis. 1966

The Lion, the Witch and the Wardrobe, C.S. Lewis, Penguin Books; New York, NY, 1950.

Chapter 17: *The Sands of Time Are Sinking*, Anne Ross Cousin, 1824-1906

Chapter 19: Chris Rice - Untitled Hymn (Come to Jesus) Lyrics | MetroLyrics

Chapter 21: *Where Does a Mother Go to Resign?* Barbara Johnson; Bethany House Publishers, Minneapolis, MN, 1994, pp. 103-104.

Systematic Theology: *An Introduction to Biblical Theology*; Wayne Grudem; Zondervan; Grand Rapids, MI, 1994, p. 810.

from the poem "All that is Gold Does Not Glitter," *The Fellowship of the Ring*, J. R. R. Tolkien, Methuen; Toronto, ON, 1956, p. 182.

Crowded to Christ, L.E. Maxwell, Wm. B. Eerdmans Publishing Co.; Grand Rapids, MI, 1950, p. 15.

Chapter 23: Comfort for Christian Parents of Unconverted Children, Jim Elliff, http://www.ccwtoday.org/article/comfort-for-christian-parents-of-unconverted-children/

Chapter 24: *The Good News We Almost Forgot*, Kevin DeYoung; Moody Publishers, Chicago, 2010, p.22.

Tabletalk magazine, Ligonier Ministries; Sanford, FL, October, 2012 ed., p. 57.

Chapter 25: *His Bright Light: The Story of Nick Traina,* Danielle Steele, Random House, Inc.: New York, NY, p.94.

A Grief Observed, C.S. Lewis, Bantam Books; New York, NY, 1961, p. 89

Chapter 26: John Milton, *Paradise Lost*, Book XI

.

Chapter 39: *Systematic Theology: An Introduction to Biblical Theology*, Wayne Grudem: Grand Rapids, MI, Zondervan, 1994, p. 810

John Piper tweet: https://l.facebook.com/l.php?u=https%3A%2F%2Ftwitter.com%2Fjohnpiper%2Fstatus%2F625116040792567808&h=GAQHr-Gxd

Emergency! True Stories from the Nation's ERs, Villard Books, New York, NY, 1996, p. 77

The Rage Against God, Peter Hitchens, Zondervan; Grand Rapids, MI, 2010, p. 41.

David Platt, https://www.thegospelcoalition.org/article/why-god-didnt-ordain-that-tragedy-is-terrible-news Dec. 2, 2013

https://www.thegospelcoalition.org/article/piper-platt-and-chandler-on-gods-goodness-in-your-pain, May 2016

Chapter 40: *Have You Seen Candace?* Wilma Derkson Tyndale House Publishers Inc.; Wheaton, IL, 1991, p. 136.

The God I Love, Joni Eareckson Tada, Zondervan Publishers; Grand Rapids, MI, 2003, p. 339.

Peace Child, Don Richardson, Regal Books; Ventura, CA, 2005, 4th ed., p. 215, 216.

Dr. Mark Hardt and Dannette Carroll, Montana State U-Billings, http://healingheart.net/articles/grief_and_divorce.html

www.ncbi.nlm.nih.gov/pmc/articles/PMC2841012/]

Chapter 41: Alice Cooper quoted on www.thegoodbook.com/christmas-playlist

Have You Seen Candace? Wilma Derkson, Tyndale House Publishers Inc.; Wheaton, IL, 1991, p. 201

https://blogs.thegospelcoalition.org/justintaylor/2016/12/07/a-woman-of-whom-the-world-was-not-worthy-helen-roseveare-1925-2016

Man's Search for Meaning, Viktor Frankl, Touchstone Publishers; Greenwich, CT, 1984, p. 55